THE SPIRIT TO SERVE

THE SPIRIT TO SERVE

Marriott's Way

J. W. MARRIOTT, JR., AND
KATHI ANN BROWN

HarperBusiness
A Division of HarperCollinsPublishers

HarperCollins books may be purchased for educational, business, or sales promotional use. For information please write: Special Markets Department, HarperCollins Publishers, Inc., 10 East 53rd Street, New York, NY 10022.

Designed by Elina D. Nudelman

Library of Congress Cataloging-in-Publication Data

Marriott, J. Willard (John Willard), 1932–
    The spirit to serve : Marriott's way / by J. W. Marriott, Jr., and Kathi Ann Brown. — 1st ed.
       p.   cm.
    Includes index.
    ISBN 0-06-662114-3
    ISBN 0-88730-991-7
    1. Hospitality industry—Management.   2. Marriott International, Inc.   I. Brown, Kathi Ann.   II. Title.
TX911.3.M27M335   1997
647.94'068—DC21   97-22874

    03 04 05 06 RRD 10

*To Dad, Mother, Donna, and
every Marriott associate*

—BILL

1957

A few minutes after the ribbon was cut to open the first Marriott hotel in January 1957, the phone rang in the freshly painted lobby. The caller asked young Bill Marriott if the Marriotts would like to buy the new 48-room Disneyland Hotel in Anaheim, California. When consulted, Bill's dad replied: "Heavens, no! We probably won't be able to make this one work."

1997

"Marriott's got 1,500 hotels in our system now, and by the year 2000, we'll reach 2,000. . . . There are probably ten million rooms in the world. Marriott has just two percent. Two percent! That's a lot of opportunity. We just have to be smart and aggressive enough to make it happen. And I think we are."

J. W. MARRIOTT, JR.
INTERVIEW: AUGUST 1997

CONTENTS

AUTHORS' NOTE

Since publication of the hardcover edition of this book in September, 1997, Marriott International, Inc. spun off to its shareholders a new public company comprised of its lodging, senior living, and distribution services businesses. This new organization adopted the Marriott International name.

Marriott's food service and facilities management business (Marriott Management Services) was then merged with the North American operations of

Sodexho Alliance to form Sodexho Marriott Services, Inc.

Today, there are four distinctly separate public companies that carry the Marriott name: Marriott International, Inc., Host Marriott Corporation, Host Marriott Services Corporation, and Sodexho Marriott Services, Inc. Each company is guided by the same principles of service and value that have been applied successfully for more than seven decades.

—June 1998

FOREWORD

I don't know how many times I've heard people say, "I would really like to start and build a successful company, but I don't have a great idea." More often than not, I remind them that if J. Willard Marriott had thought the same thing, the Marriott enterprise would not exist today. I enjoy telling them the story of how he began not with a great idea or a brilliant strategy, but with the simple desire to build something from the ground up and—most important—build it to last.

From the small acorn of a single A&W Root Beer franchise—hardly the invention of electricity or the personal computer—has grown the mighty oak of today's Marriott.

Like all enduring great companies, Marriott's lasting success does not come from a single great idea, brilliant strategy, lucky break, or even a single great leader. Each of these advantages—even if a company has them—does not last forever. No, the foundations of a great company lie in more fundamental attributes. As Jerry Porras and I wrote in our book *Built to Last: Successful Habits of Visionary Companies*, the culmination of our six-year study into what makes enduring great companies, Marriott attained its stature because it shares in common certain timeless fundamentals found in such companies as Procter & Gamble, Hewlett-Packard, 3M, and Nordstrom.

1. *Timeless core values and enduring purpose.* Truly great companies maintain a set of core values and a core purpose that remain fixed while their business strategies and practices continually adapt to a changing world. They understand the difference between what should never change and what should be open for change, between what is truly sacred and what is not.

   As with all great companies, Marriott's core values did not come from intellectualizing with business school professors, following fads, or listening to the rantings of management gurus. Marriott's core values can be traced back over seventy years to the *personal* core values of J. Willard Marriott, who wove them into the fabric of the company and then passed them along to his son Bill Marriott, Jr. There can be no distinction between a company's core values and the core values of its leadership. The values originate from deep inside the people themselves—authentic, bone deep, passionately held. Marriott's core values—including the belief that people are number one ("Take care of Marriott people and they will take care of Marriott guests"), a commitment to continuous improvement and overcoming adversity, and a good old-fashioned dedication to hard work and having fun while doing it—provide a foundation of stability and enduring character.

Similarly, the company's core purpose—to make people away from home feel that they are among friends and are really wanted—serves as a fixed point of guidance and inspiration. Broad enough to stimulate strategic change over time (from Hot Shoppes to airline catering to hotels to senior living communities to who knows what in the next century), this purpose can also guide strategic thinking about what *not* to do. Perhaps most important, this purpose provides inspiration by making clear that the company exists for more fundamental reasons than just making money. Of course, it must make money, too. Great companies generate substantial wealth, but great companies do not let the pursuit of profit divert them from their central purpose. Marriott has done its best when it has kept this lesson in mind. As Mr. Marriott writes in these pages, the company has gone astray when it has lost sight of its basic purpose.

Marriott's status as a great company in the next century depends directly upon how well it continues to live up to its core values and purpose while simultaneously stimulating change and progress in everything else. The company may evolve far beyond its current lines of business in the next 100 years, but to remain great, it must simultaneously remain passionately dedicated to these timeless principles no matter how much it grows or what new opportunities it pursues.

2. *A relentless drive for progress.* Core values and purpose alone cannot make a company great. It must also have an unceasing drive to change, improve, and renew itself. As Will Rogers was

fond of saying, "Even if you're on the right track, you'll get run over if you just sit there."

From the earliest days of the company, the Marriotts demonstrated an innate aversion to sitting still. The drive that propelled the company from a single Hot Shoppe to a multibillion-dollar global company came not from the desire to attain the trappings of success but from the passion for growth and improvement *for its own sake*.

In the early 1960s, Bill Marriott, Jr., commented that he hoped the company would one day be as successful as Howard Johnson, which at the time far exceeded Marriott in sales and national renown. Where is Howard Johnson today? Why has Marriott so far surpassed the vast majority of its competitors from decades past and become one of the leading corporations in the entire world? For a simple reason: While the inheritors of successful family businesses often rest on the laurels of their parents, Bill Marriott, Jr., went around putting big sharp thorns in the Marriott laurels, making it uncomfortable if not impossible to rest. The guest satisfaction scorecards, the management by walking around, the customer secret shoppers, and all the other mechanisms—self-imposed thorns—created a stimulus for self-improvement.

Bill Marriott, Jr., himself could have easily retired years ago, settling into a leisurely lifestyle of wealth and comfort. But he didn't, for the spirit of Marriott lies in the concept that there is no finish line, no ultimate summit, no "having made it."

As Bill Marriott, Jr., outlines in these pages, Marriott has on occasion found itself off course when it allowed this relentless discipline to wane, but brought itself back on track by reinvigorating it. The litmus test of a company's enduring greatness comes not only from its track record of success but from its ability to bounce back from setbacks, failures, and difficult times. No company has a perfect, unblemished track record; all have dark days at some point in their history. The critical variable is *resiliency*, not perfection. In my view, the best pages of this book do not concentrate on the success stories of Marriott, but the acknowledgment of mistakes and the learning gained from them. Marriott at its best does not dwell on the question, "How well have we done?" but on the question, "How can we do better tomorrow than we did today?" This attitude of humility, along with the constant search for new challenges, commitment to audacious goals, learning from successes and failures, and belief that good enough never is, will enable the company to remain great into the next century and beyond.

3. *Strength beyond the presence of any one individual.* Finally, Marriott demonstrates the crucial distinction between a company with visionary leadership and a visionary company. J. Willard Marriott was a remarkable man, yet the company ultimately did not depend on him. Bill Marriott, Jr., also displays remarkable characteristics, but the company is much more than the visionary leadership of a single individual. In the very act of writing this book, he demonstrates his desire to pass his wisdom along so that the company can prosper far beyond his daily presence. The sign of a great company builder lies not in being indispensable but in building a company that will surpass itself in subsequent generations. J. Willard Marriott did just that, and Bill Marriott, Jr., displays the same ambition.

The next generation of Marriott management will, I hope, share the same core values and purpose that have guided the company for seventy years and *simultaneously* exhibit the drive to continually change and improve operating practices and business strategies. For the key to prospering and adapting in the coming decades amidst an ever-escalating rate of change is to first be clear about and resolutely dedicated to what you stand for and why that should never change. You must then be just as resolutely willing to change absolutely everything else. This rare ability to manage continuity and change is the secret of Marriott's past—and the key to its future.

Jim Collins
Boulder, Colorado
September 1997

PREFACE

Experience is not what happens to a man; it is what a man does with what happens to him.

—ALDOUS HUXLEY

In every large hotel—hidden from the eyes and ears of guests—exists an invisible city. Behind doors, below ground, a maze of corridors connects kitchens to loading docks, housekeeping to the laundry, accounting to the communications center. An around-the-clock army of cooks, housekeepers, engineers, waiters, dishwashers, electricians, and other specialists bustle along these hallways, each member responsible for making his or her part of hotel operations run smoothly.

The lodging industry has a special term to describe this hidden world. We call it the "heart of the house."

Like hotels, every company has its "heart of the house." There, the hurly-burly of product creation, manufacturing, marketing, finance, and dozens of other vital functions takes place, largely unseen by customers and clients. Ideas are tried and discarded; decisions are debated, made, regretted, corrected; systems are fine-tuned; careers rise and fall. And with luck, a few lessons are learned along the way.

I've been working in the heart of Marriott's house for more than forty years. During that time, the organization has grown from a $50 million restaurant and airline catering chain with one hotel into a $12 billion global company managing more than 1,500 hotels, resorts, and time-share properties; dozens of senior living communities; and thousands of food service contracts and other special services. To give you a sense of scale, we probably prepare more meals and make up more beds each day than anyone except the U.S. Army. I'd be a liar if I pretended not to be extremely proud of what we've built on the foundation of my father's original A&W Root Beer stand, launched in 1927.

The path leading to today's Marriott has not been entirely smooth, of course. We've done quite a few things right—some of which you'll read about in these pages—but we've also made our share of mistakes.

Most of them have been pretty small, but some have been real whoppers. You'll also read about a few of these.

You might wonder why I would intentionally shine a spotlight on the places where we've stubbed (or even chopped off) our toes. Why emphasize the negative when it would be a snap to celebrate the triumphs and sidestep the failures?

That's easy. Successes *and* failures both have a great deal to teach. And I wanted this book, above all, to be about learning.

So as you turn the pages, don't expect to be treated to a full-blown, star-spangled history of Marriott. I've highlighted only key episodes from our past. Nor will you find a how-to-succeed-in-business textbook filled with new and improved management ideas. I leave that to the gurus of our nation's business schools.

What you will find are a few simple, plainspoken lessons about "the spirit to serve" that I've learned over the course of a lifetime in business at Marriott. They're lessons grounded largely in common sense, tested by time, and taught by that wisest and most eloquent of all teachers: experience.

J. W. MARRIOTT, JR.
Bethesda, Maryland
September 1997

Personally, I'm always ready to learn,
although I do not always like being taught.

—Winston Churchill

THE SPIRIT TO SERVE

1

ROAD-TESTED RESEARCH: THE BENEFITS OF BEING A HANDS-ON MANAGER

"The true test of civilization," declared American essayist Ralph Waldo Emerson in 1870, "is not the census, nor the size of cities, nor the crops—no, but the kind of man the country turns out."

I'd like to offer a contemporary twist on Emerson's noble thought. That is, the true test of a *company* is the kind of *manager* it turns out. Naturally, I'd like to think that Marriott passes this test hands down.

I recently spent the better part of a day with a

Marriott associate who fits my notion of the kind of manager our company should aspire to produce. He's the general manager of one of our largest convention hotel properties. As GM, he's essentially the captain of the ship. As we toured the property together, this fellow radiated energy and enthusiasm. He knew every inch of the hotel and grounds, and he never missed a beat answering my detailed questions.

Happy as I was with the hotel's "numbers"—guest satisfaction scores, occupancy rates, profitability, etc.—I was even more delighted by the interaction between the hotel's staff and the GM as we strolled the heart of the house and public areas. Not only did he know every staff member of this mini-city by sight—*without* checking name tags—but better yet, he was greeted by smiles, teasing, and hellos from just about every Marriott associate we passed.

What's the big deal? Why was I so pleased?

At Marriott, the reaction of staff to the GM is the ultimate litmus test of how well a hotel is run. The same goes for any of our managers in any division of the company. If employees are tickled to see the boss, I know that he or she is a great *hands-on* manager. Only someone who spends much of the day strolling the hallways or property talking to employees and taking their concerns to heart earns such a friendly greeting.

Why is it so important that our managers be out on the floor all day and not holed up in an office? If a manager is hands-on, more than likely she's also on top of her business. She can pick up immediately on problems, concerns, or issues and take care of them before they fester or grow. Conversely, a manager who doesn't know his staff by name, who doesn't spend the bulk of the day walking the heart of the house, will eventually have problems. He's just not going to have the same rapport with associates or the knowledge base to make decisions as do his hands-on counterparts.

That's why when I come across a GM who excites his or her employees like the fellow at the big convention hotel, I'm excited, too. We've got a long-term winner—for the property, associates, guests, and company. I'm especially gratified if I discover that the GM grew up, so to speak, in the Marriott system. Someone who has learned to be a good hands-on manager while at Marriott is the best test of our company's management philosophy. It tells me that after seventy years, our original corporate culture is still going strong.

The hands-on, management-by-walking-around approach became a Marriott tradition the moment the doors of our first root beer stand opened on May 20, 1927. My father, J. Willard Marriott, was the ultimate hands-on manager. He visited his restaurants almost

3

every day, often with my younger brother Dick and me in tow. Of course, as a kid, I just thought we were going out to eat. As I got older, I caught on to what Dad was up to. To him, the best way—the only way— to know what was really going on in his business was to see it and hear it with his own eyes and ears.

My father's hands-on attitude wasn't limited to inspecting, correcting, or approving. When we opened our very first hotel (Twin Bridges, Arlington, Virginia) in January 1957, Mother, Dad, and I stayed up half the night hanging pictures so we could check in guests the next day in time for President Eisenhower's second inauguration.

Some of my own earliest experiences working for the company were also literally hands-on. When I took on the assignment of shepherding our second hotel (Key Bridge, Arlington, Virginia) into existence in 1958, I was responsible for everything from hiring the architect and designing the hotel to securing the general contractor for construction to putting together the team we needed to get the hotel up and running on opening day. If I thought that in pulling off such a tall order I'd outgrown my days of picture-hanging, I soon learned otherwise. The week before our first Philadelphia hotel opened on City Line Avenue in 1961, I was down on my knees gluing rubber base-board into place in the lobby.

Those early experiences—and thousands more in the forty years since—reinforced my conviction that there's simply no substitute for being hands-on if you truly want to understand your business.

Not everyone is comfortable in the spotlight, I know, but every manager and business leader ought to at least give the hands-on approach a try. Pretend you don't have a desk or an office for a week or just a couple of days. You might discover that you've been missing out on a wealth of opportunities to connect with employees and customers, assess your businesses firsthand, and spot new ways of improving customer and associate satisfaction.

The time I spend on the road—actually, some 150,000 air miles a year—visiting Marriott locations is invaluable to me. One of the most important things it allows me to do is counter the notion that big corporations are faceless machines. If you're in the service business and your name is above the door, it's important for people to be able to link a face to the name. I want our associates to know that there really *is* a guy named Marriott who cares about them, even if he can only drop by every so often to personally tell them so.

I also want to show our team in the field that I value their work enough to take the time to check it out. Without their help, Marriott not only wouldn't be Marriott, Marriott wouldn't *be*, period. So I *do* get down on the floor in hotel rooms and check under the beds. I open dresser drawers; switch on faucets, showers, and lamps; and peek in closets to see if there's an iron and ironing board and enough hangers.

Visits are not limited to the public areas. I head for the heart of the house, too. I check out the laundry, accounting, kitchen, and any other corners that I think merit a quick look. There's method to my madness. If I see smiling faces and well-scrubbed surfaces behind the scenes, I know that the rest of the hotel more than likely is doing just fine.

Unlike my father, who had a habit of dropping in at the Hot Shoppes, I rarely show up at Marriott locations unannounced. I often visit as many as ten locations in a single day, so I want to make every minute count. But letting people know that I'm coming for a visit occasionally has its humorous downsides. Over the years, I've become an old hand at recognizing last-minute the-boss-is-coming freshening up. Especially new coats of paint. I carry paint remover in my overnight kit to make short work of the inevitable spots on my suits that result from good intentions.

In addition to keeping me connected to Marriott's associates, my visits teach me volumes about what's working out in the field. I can't think of a single tour in all the years I've been on the road that didn't teach me something. I'm constantly impressed by the ingenuity of our associates. I invariably return home with stacks of index cards filled with ideas about things that we should be doing or things that are out of whack and need fixing. Those ideas quickly find their way into the hands of members of the team at headquarters who can either solve the problem or spread the word about a good concept that works.

I would say, in fact, that one of the most rewarding things about being so close to every aspect of Marriott's business is watching great ideas cross-fertilize. Marriott's first experiment in promoting brand names (a.k.a. "branding"), for example, came at our toll-road restaurants back in the 1970s. Eager to breathe new life into a few older, lackluster turnpike facilities, we switched them over to our Roy Rogers and Big Boy restaurant brands. Sales took off! Travelers enjoyed the comfort of knowing that they could pull off the road on a long trip and sit down to a familiar menu.

In due time, the folks in Marriott's airport concession business took note of the success of their counterparts in toll roads and adapted the idea to fit their customers' needs. We hooked up first with Pizza Hut, followed by other recognized fast-food brands, and soon our airport concession business was also enjoying a boom in sales, thanks to the power of branding.

My only real role in Marriott's original branding

experiment was giving the official nod, but it's been great seeing the concept succeed, catch fire, and spread. Today, our entire lodging division, for example, is organized under a "brand management" structure. Best of all, I like knowing that it was the hands-on, always-alert-to-opportunity attitude of managers in both toll-road and airport concessions that allowed that original idea to take hold and flourish.

Visiting Marriott locations year in and year out has also provided me with a strong knowledge base for making decisions. Because I'm constantly involved in the day-to-day aspects of the business, our staff knows that if they come to me with a concern or idea, they're usually not going to have to spend a lot of time getting me up to speed. They can normally get my yea or nay readily and take action quickly.

For example, a few years ago, Marriott's time-share division (Marriott Vacation Club International, or MVCI) presented their budget for converting the old Custom House in downtown Boston. I liked the concept, but the economics of the project were thin. The property's views of Boston Harbor from rooms on the upper floors brought to mind the breathtaking "rooms with a view" that I had visited not long before at an oceanfront Marriott in Kauai, Hawaii. The Pacific-view rooms naturally commanded a higher rate. The parallel was obvious. Why not charge a little more for the upper-floor rooms with a splendid harbor view in the Custom House? We quickly adopted a differential pricing structure for our harbor-view rooms, and the financial picture brightened accordingly.

An example on a much larger scale is a decision we made to sell off the fine-dining operations of two food service companies Marriott acquired in the 1980s. Marriott had been in the restaurant business for nearly six decades at that point and had had its own fine-dining operations in the past. I knew enough about the business from personal, frontline experience to know that we didn't want to wrestle with that category again. So when we purchased the giant food service purveyor Saga Corporation for $700 million in 1986, we immediately sold off its restaurants for $350 million. If we had not already had our own hands-on experience with fine dining, we might have lost time and a lot of money trying to make those restaurants work instead of quickly passing them on to someone eager to take them off our hands.

Sometimes it takes us a *little* longer to see the light. But once we do, we try to move fast. About a decade ago, we took a fresh look at our sixty-year-old internal distribution system and realized that we were sitting on top of a potential new external business. Since the days of the Hot Shoppes, we had been handling our own shipping of food and supplies among Marriott properties. With so many locations and a yearly grocery tab destined to grow into hundreds of millions of dollars, it had made economic sense to cultivate an in-house distribution capability. What didn't occur to us for a long time was the potential for selling this distribution experience to others. The lightbulb went on when we discovered that our costs were lower than our competitors. This realization, combined with our in-depth knowledge of the distribution business, gave us the confidence to move quickly to sign up outside clients for Marriott Distribution Services (MDS). External customers now supply more than half the annual sales for MDS.

Another big benefit of being hands-on is what the marketplace can teach you free of charge. Nothing replaces listening to your own customers firsthand. Not only will you find out what you're doing right and wrong, you might just pick up an idea for a brand-new product or business.

Marriott's former In-Flite airline catering division was the result of one such exercise by my father. In 1937, while visiting the Hot Shoppe adjacent to the old Hoover airfield on the outskirts of Washington, he noticed customers buying sandwiches and hot coffee to take with them. A little Q and A got to the heart of the matter. Travelers wanted to eat on the plane.

Dad soon flew to Miami to propose an onboard

meal program to Eastern Air Transport's chief, Eddie Rickenbacker, and what would at one point be the world's largest airline catering business was born. All because my father was on the scene and had his eyes open to new opportunities.

The incubation of Courtyard by Marriott in the early 1980s is another good example of how keeping your eyes and ears open in the marketplace can make for good business. Until Courtyard's debut, Marriott had focused only on the full-service hotel business. Other segments were new territory for us. When we decided to go after the moderate-priced hotel segment, we pulled out all the stops. We wanted to know exactly what we were up against. Our small, fanatically dedicated Courtyard team scattered to the four winds, checking out the competition by literally checking *in* to their hotels for a firsthand look. Team members spent hundreds of nights sitting in competitors' hotel rooms taking detailed notes about furnishings, room arrangements, and service. They also interviewed business travelers to learn what *they* wanted in a hotel room. The information gathered was critical to the fresh concept and design of Courtyard by Marriott.

Like the Courtyard team, my own hands-on practice also includes intense information gathering . . . *inside* Marriott's four walls. I don't hesitate to call down into our organization several levels to hear different view-points or make a quick query. I suspect this particular tic occasionally turns the place upside down, sending people running in all directions to get me answers, but it's a good idea to fight the hierarchy and bureaucracy that creep into any organization that has as many employees as we do. I also firmly believe that both the company and I benefit from knowing that I'm only a casual phone call away from any point in the organization.

Working for someone who is a true believer in the hands-on philosophy isn't always easy. I know—I worked for my father for almost thirty years. In spite of what I've just said about my own hands-on style, I'd like to think that our staff today has it a little bit easier than my dad's Hot Shoppes managers forty years ago.

Back in the heyday of the Hot Shoppes, the daily menu had more than 300 items on it. My father insisted that every selection be available—and fresh—at all times. Naturally, this is virtually impossible in the restaurant business, but Dad would not hear otherwise. If he went into a Hot Shoppe and they were out of something, he'd raise the roof. After a few such instances, the managers took matters into their own hands. When my dad showed up at a shop and ordered something that wasn't available, the kitchen would call the nearest Hot Shoppe to see if they had it.

If they did, runners from the two restaurants would meet in the middle to rush the order back to my unsuspecting father.

Pretty ingenious, eh? I'm still trying to decide if that's an example of "hands-on" or "*hand*-off" management. Whatever you call it, there are moments during my whirlwind property tours when I feel a close kinship with those Hot Shoppes runners. Being on my feet all day and truly running from location to location to stay on schedule can leave me wiped out at the close of business. But even as I'm easing gratefully into a hot shower at day's end, I know I wouldn't trade my time on the run for the most comfortable desk chair in the world.

The truth is, I'm still having fun after forty years.

2

THE DEVIL IS IN THE DETAILS—SUCCESS IS IN THE SYSTEMS

A little neglect may breed great mischief . . . for want of a nail the shoe is lost, for want of a shoe the horse is lost, for want of a horse the rider is lost.

—BEN FRANKLIN

When my wife, Donna, and I were first married forty-some years ago, my father would visit our house and—like clockwork—run his index finger over the furniture, doorsills, and venetian blinds checking for dust.

Needless to say, this drove my wife nuts.

I had it even worse. Donna merely married into Dad's perfectionism; I was *born* into it. When I was a child, one of my regular chores was to shine my father's shoes on Saturday so they would be pristine for church on Sunday. I can still recall one long afternoon spent sitting in the bathroom with my mother, scrubbing furiously at some kind of awful, black gummy stuff that Dad had picked up on his soles during his travels that week. It took us hours to clean that junk off, but we did it. And I learned a lasting lesson in sticking with a job until it's done right.

As you might imagine, my father was a challenge to live with. And just as exacting to work for. He was never satisfied with anything. Perfection was one notch below desired result.

When he visited the company's restaurants and hotels, it was the same story. There was a specified way of doing things, and heaven help employees who caught my father's eye when they weren't following Marriott's standard operating procedures (SOPs). More than one Hot Shoppes cook, I'm sure, was stunned to find the chairman of the board standing by his side, testing him on how many times hash brown potatoes should be turned on the grill. If the reply was anything but "once," you can bet my dad quizzed that employee to exhaustion about every other aspect of the job, suspicious about what other procedures the poor fellow may have been ignoring.

I'm more readily satisfied than my father ever was. But like him, I do believe that there's a right way and a wrong way of doing things—and doing things the right way is worth making a habit. This includes taking care of the smallest details. If the devil is in the details, as has often been said, then that's clearly where it pays to pay the closest attention.

We are sometimes teased about our passion for the Marriott Way of doing things. If you happen to work in the hospitality industry, you might already be familiar with our encyclopedic procedural manuals, which include what is probably the most infamous of the bunch: a guide setting out sixty-six separate steps for cleaning a hotel room in less than half an hour.

Maybe we *are* a little fanatical about the way things should be done. But for us, the idea of having systems and procedures for everything is very natural and logical: If you want to produce a consistent result, you need to figure out how to do it, write it down, practice it, and keep improving it until there's nothing left to improve. (Of course, we at Marriott believe that there's *always* something to improve.)

Why do we feel that doing things consistently is so important? The simple answer is that it's the solid foundation upon which virtually every aspect of Marriott rests. If we've got our systems down cold, everything else becomes that much easier.

Think about it for a moment. At the most basic level, systems help bring order to the natural messiness of human enterprise. Give 100 people the same task—without providing ground rules—and you'll end up with at least a dozen, if not 100, different ways of doing it. Try that same experiment with a few thousand people, and you end up with chaos. Efficient systems and clear rules help everyone to deliver a *consistent* product and service.

In the contract services and lodging businesses—at least in our eyes—consistency is the name of the game. Mr. Emerson, whom I quoted in Chapter 1, once disparaged "foolish consistency" as the "hobgoblin of little minds." Mindless conformity and the thoughtful setting of standards should never be confused. In our case, the latter has proved to be one of the main engines of our success.

One of our chief aims is to provide our customers with service free of hassles and surprises. Road-tested systems and SOPs make this possible by taking the element of surprise out of situations where surprise is the last thing a guest wants. We try to provide a level of service so dependable that a guest can land on our doorstep virtually asleep on her feet and not miss a "zzz" while we register and usher her to a room for the night.

That level of consistency gives customers confidence in your brand name and an incentive to come back again and again. We could not have expanded as quickly, widely, or profitably as we have over the years if we had had to reinvent the wheel every time we unveiled a new hotel, resort, restaurant, or senior living community. Or if we were forced to reintroduce ourselves to the world each time a new facility opened. Many guests at our newest properties come because they've already experienced Marriott elsewhere. Customers probably don't spend a moment thinking about it, but it's partly our systems and SOPs that bring them back.

Systems have been deeply ingrained for so long in our corporate culture that I'm always a little surprised when I come across companies that aren't as devoted to them as we are. Among our peers in the hospitality industry, I often see wasted opportunities to improve performance, simply because no one seems to be focusing on developing, much less implementing and maintaining, systems and standards. The result is uneven, unreliable, and often unremarkable service. Perhaps you've already discovered this in your travels when you've stayed at two hotels that share the same name, yet you experienced vastly different levels of quality in rooms and service.

Marriott has developed chain-wide systems and safety nets to try to prevent that from happening. When you walk into a full-service Marriott hotel in downtown Washington, you'll be treated to the same basic experience you would get if you were checking in to the Los Angeles Airport Marriott three time zones away. A Residence Inn in Minneapolis will offer the same amenities that you've come to expect from the one located just down the street from your best client in Santa Clara, California. Each Marriott brand has its own heart-of-the-house systems and SOPs that define and promote consistency across the brand.

Those systems and safety nets didn't appear overnight, of course. Undergirding and shaping them is seventy-plus years of detail-obsessed Marriott corporate culture. Like our hands-on management philosophy, Marriott's pursuit of consistency goes back to our Hot Shoppes roots in the late 1920s. Almost from the start, my parents—especially my father—launched the process of figuring out how to do something right and then writing it down. From washing windows to burnishing silverware to arranging buffet tables and processing customers' checks, no aspect of the workplace went untouched by my dad's penchant for systemization.

One of Marriott's earliest and longest-lived SOPs is our recipe card system, originally developed for us by a professional dietitian in the 1940s. In her specially built test kitchen, Mrs. Savage would experiment with new Hot Shoppes dishes and come up with the best recipes for large-quantity preparation. Recipe cards became SOP in our hotel restaurants, too. Anyone who deviated from Mrs. Savage's instructions—or worse, didn't have the card out in clear view when preparing a dish—was sure to provoke a sharp-tongued lecture from my father.

You might think that by the time I came on board with the company in the mid–1950s, there was no room for improvement in our systems. By then we'd been in business thirty years. Dad, of course, would never have agreed. My first full-time job with Marriott was in food service; my main task was to continue to beef up our food service standards.

Although I had just completed a tour with the Navy as a supply officer on the U.S.S. *Randolph*, Marriott still had plenty to teach me about efficiency. I spent the first few months on the job figuring out how to eliminate slow-ups in Hot Shoppes service due to lack of plates, dishes, silverware, and so on. My job also included a constant hunt for ways to shave seconds off the time it took to process a food order, from the moment it arrived in the kitchen to the moment a waitress served the dish to the customer.

My budding career in food service ended abruptly when I asked Dad to let me get involved with managing our brand-new hotel "division." (Division? We had one hotel up and running in 1957!) In contrast to Hot Shoppes, systems were few and far between on the hotel side of the business.

Maybe I should have been more daunted by our lack of experience in lodging, but truth be told, it was terrific fun. We were flying by the seat of our pants, thrilled and a little surprised by our own moxie. We didn't exactly start out modestly. Our first hotel, Twin Bridges, was a sprawling complex of 365 rooms. Our second, Key Bridge, had more than 200 rooms to start. Virtually before the original paint dried, we added more rooms and public spaces to both hotels and began planning our third and fourth.

We were able to transfer a few systems from the Hot Shoppes to the hotels, but it was really the transfer of *attitude* about systems that counted most. The whole time we were fussing, fiddling, experimenting, and generally mucking around with our first few properties, we were also diligently jotting down every idea that seemed to work, slowly building from the ground up not only our hotels but also the systems to run them.

I remember starting room service from scratch at Twin Bridges, about four months after the hotel opened. Talk about a hands-on, making-it-up-as-you-go-along experience. I had just officially moved over from the food service side of the company. At the end of my first month on the new job, I found myself putting together room service trays and filling guest orders myself. Not that I was any kind of expert on the subject! I quickly trained two or three other people, and they took it from there.

Keeping costs under control was another challenge. My very first "executive decision" involved, of all things, ice buckets. I was looking over our expenses for Twin Bridges a few weeks into the operation and noticed a pretty hefty sum under the category "Other." A little investigation revealed that guests found our plastic-covered, cardboard ice buckets so sturdy and convenient that they were filling them up with ice and drinks to take on the road. At a dollar apiece, the loss of thousands of buckets in a year would have quickly eaten up our meager profits. (Average room rate in 1957 was $9 a night!) I then ordered permanent ice buckets to be placed in each room, and we were back in business.

Earlier, I credited Marriott's systems and SOPs with being the "solid foundation" of the entire corporation. You may be wondering if knowing how to cook hash browns, run room service, and substitute permanent ice buckets *really* qualifies for so lofty a status. Perhaps you've been waiting for the inside scoop on inventory, payroll, and accounting?

We have plenty of administrative systems, of course. And cutting-edge finance has definitely played a part in our story. But the best administrative and financial systems in the world wouldn't have gotten us very far if we hadn't had something to sell. In Marriott's case, our principal product is probably not what you think it is. Yes, we're in the food-and-lodging business (among other things). Yes, we "sell" room nights, food and beverage, and time-shares. But what we're really selling is our *expertise in managing the processes that make those sales possible*. And that expertise rests firmly on our mastery of thousands of tiny operational details.

Let me explain. If you're not in the hospitality industry, you might not be aware that the mainstream chain hotels you stay in are rarely owned by the company whose name is on the building. As of 1997, Marriott owns outright only about a half dozen of the more than 1,500 hotels that bear the Marriott logo. By the time we reach our goal of 2,000 hotels by the year 2000, our proportion of ownership will be less than 1 of every 100 hotels in our global system.

Many of the most recent additions to our lodging system have come from franchising the Marriott brands. But from the late 1970s until the early 1990s, our primary growth in lodging came from building and selling hotels to investors and taking back long-term (often seventy-five-year) *management contracts*. Between 1978 and 1990, we boosted the number of our guest rooms from about 20,000 to more than

150,000, each year increasing the proportion of rooms under management by Marriott but not owned by the company itself.

I won't explain here why that particular financing method made sense for us; my aim is simply to highlight the fact that Marriott's major selling point—the fuel for our growth since 1978—has been our ability to show investors that we know what we're doing when it comes to running a hotel. That's where the hash browns, room service, and ice buckets (plus thousands of other details) come into play. All of our intense attention to detail translates into consistent quality. Consistent quality leads to high customer satisfaction. Customer satisfaction translates into high occupancy, repeat business, and good room rates. Those in turn bring home good profits and attractive returns to the property owners.

In short, if we couldn't produce high customer satisfaction, none of the rest would follow. Marriott probably wouldn't have 100 hotels, much less 1,500, under its various flags. Only by being able to show our investors that we have what it takes to run a profitable hotel with a strong customer base can we win their confidence . . . and long-term management contracts. So when I say that the company's prosperity rests on such things as our sixty-six-steps-to-clean-a-room manual, I'm not exaggerating.

Our operational skills were also what saved us when the hotel industry ran into trouble at the beginning of the 1990s. Marriott, like many lodging companies, got caught in the real estate crash that kicked off the decade. One of the principal things that helped us make it through the tough times was our long-haul track record in managing profitable hotels and contract services. In order to ride out the economic downturn, we had to maintain customer and investor confidence in our fundamental strength. Our terrific folks in operations, plus our tried-and-true systems, helped pull our fat out of the fire by maintaining consistent results in customer satisfaction.

Now that I've praised systems and SOPs to the skies, let me talk a little bit about what they *don't* do. Even the most maniacally detailed procedures can't cover every situation, problem, or emergency that might arise. The quirkiness of life simply doesn't allow for it. And I'm not sure that it would be such a good idea if it did. Things would be pretty boring.

What solid systems and SOPs do is nip *common* problems in the bud so that staff can focus instead on solving the *un*common problems that come their way. In a service industry, that—plus a bias for action—is the key to success. By nailing the basics into place, systems allow employees to provide more customized customer service. They can just get on with the job of delivering the kind of quality attention that distinguishes extraordinary from ordinary.

As important as it is to Marriott to strive for a level of consistency that allows customers to depend on us, we also don't want to let consistency turn into *rigidity*. A guest who gets sick in the middle of the night, for example, doesn't want to wait around while a desk clerk looks up the right SOP for the situation. She just wants to get to the hospital. The same goes for a guest whose car was towed from a downtown parking lot, or who left his passport in room 303 and is now calling from an airport courtesy phone, panicked about making his international flight. There is no SOP for the guest who sheepishly appears at the front desk twice a day because he keeps misplacing his electronic keycard. Just a little humor, compassion, and a new card.

During my lifetime with the company, I've heard hundreds of stories about extra-mile customer service that Marriott associates have provided to our guests. And those are just the ones I've been told; I know that there are thousands more. I'm never surprised—but always delighted—by what I hear. To me, it's yet another sign that our corporate culture is thriving.

Let me share a couple of stories to show you what I mean.

The first involves a woman who came to stay at one

of our smaller properties to attend a week-long national conference nearby. She was scheduled to give the first big speech of her career on the second day of the meeting. Things got off to a rocky start soon after check-in when she realized that she'd left both the battery and the power cord of her laptop computer at home. She desperately wanted to make last-minute revisions to her speech. One of our part-time associates, who's a bit of a computer jock on the side, managed to find exactly the cord she needed.

No sooner was the guest back in business than the laptop's hard drive crashed, a victim of age. Her speech was now less than twenty-four hours away, and everything seemed to be going wrong. Not to fear. Someone in the hotel's accounting department found an empty terminal and desk for her and coached her through the revision process. By the time they finished and printed out the new version of the speech, they were fast friends. The accountant pulled a couple of colleagues who were just finishing up their shifts into a small meeting room to act as an audience for a quick rehearsal. Then the same group used their lunch break the next day to play the role of smiling supporters as the guest finally (and flawlessly) delivered her talk before a packed room. I defy anyone to write an SOP to cover *that*!

The second story is one of my favorites, and one

that never fails to move me and make me very proud of Marriott. It's not often that a company gets to play fairy godmother.

A few years ago, one of our guest representatives received a call from a bride-to-be who wanted to schedule her honeymoon at one of Marriott's Caribbean resorts. When he checked back with her to discuss specific dates and room availability, she sadly told him that her fiancé had just been diagnosed with terminal brain cancer and had only a few months to live. They planned to marry anyway, but were going to have to move the wedding up to accommodate his chemotherapy. Unfortunately, the only seven-day stretch of time available for their honeymoon fell during a black-out period for the resort. There didn't seem to be any solution, so the woman thanked the guest representative for his help and hung up.

Touched by the woman's dilemma, the associate called the GM at the resort and explained the situation. The GM not only approved the reservation but upgraded their accommodations. The bride was thrilled. Then, just when it looked like things were on track, the woman called back in tears to thank Marriott for its efforts, but to say that the airline couldn't get the couple to the resort during the scheduled week.

Not satisfied with the turn of events, the guest representative called another airline and told the couple's story. Even though the airline wasn't one of our Marriott Miles travel program partners, it happily agreed to fly the honeymooners to the resort—first class and on a complimentary basis. Not to be outdone, we likewise comped the couple their room.

About four months later, our guest representative who had made all the arrangements received a thank-you letter from the woman. The couple had married and enjoyed a wonderful honeymoon. Not long after, her husband had died. Just before his death, he told his wife about how precious their time together on the island had been to him. She closed her letter by saying: "You'll never know what you and Marriott did for us."

That second story alone is proof enough for me that there are times when no rule, no system, no SOP can possibly fill the bill. The only display of "consistency" appropriate to the situation was our associate's determination to help the couple enjoy their honeymoon.

Besides, there are times when a preoccupation with consistency can be a double-edged sword. I refer to Marriott's relatively late embrace of hotel franchising.

Much of Marriott's most recent growth in lodging has come from franchising. We weren't always so enthusiastic about the idea. My father, perfectionist to the core, was not a fan of the concept. He saw what had happened to the Howard Johnson chain in the 1930s and 1940s when they franchised their restaurants widely and lost control of the situation. Among other things, the company failed to enforce strict, uniform standards of maintenance, food, and service. As a result, HoJo's restaurants went downhill and the brand name lost its luster. My father wasn't about to risk having the same thing happen to him!

Dad's reluctance kept Marriott out of serious hotel franchising until the 1990s, with good and bad results. The downside of waiting so long to take a wholehearted plunge into franchising is that we missed out on valuable expansion opportunities for a couple of decades.

The upside is that the delay gave us ample time to develop a solid track record as operators so that affiliation with the company's brand is more valuable to our franchisees now than it might otherwise have been. We have also been able to develop systems to help our franchisees understand what we expect of them. And we've had the opportunity to develop truly franchise-friendly products like Fairfield Inn, Fairfield Suites, Courtyard, and TownePlace Suites—all of which are relatively easy to run compared to a full-service hotel.

As Marriott continues to grow in the United States and abroad—whether by franchising, acquisitions, conversions, or ground-up construction—the company's strong systems and SOPs will remain a basic building block of expansion. Given our current goal to place more than 2,000 hotels under the Marriott flag by the year 2000, we'll be counting on our time-tested systems more than ever to maintain quality and consistency across all of our brand names. Knowing our affection for perfection, I suspect we will also carry on our never-ending search for ways not only to maintain but to improve our products, service, and ourselves. To that end, I hope we'll keep in mind inventor Thomas Edison's sage caution: "Show me a thoroughly satisfied man—and I will show you a failure." Or as my dad (quoting Winston Churchill) *loved* to say: "Success is never final."

3

GIVE TO YOUR EMPLOYEES—AND THEY'LL GIVE BACK TO YOU

Treat people as if they were what they ought to be and you help them to become what they are capable of being.

—Johann Wolfgang von Goethe

In 1990, Marriott laid off more than 1,000 people, most of them in two divisions at our corporate headquarters. If you think it's odd to open a chapter about taking care of employees with a story about a layoff, stay with me. I'll explain.

If you followed the business pages in the early 1990s, you might recall that Marriott went through some tough times from 1990 to 1993. The company had been on a roll throughout the 1980s—building hundreds of hotels, selling them to investors, and negotiating long-term management contracts. We had hit upon a formula for expansion that was tailor-made for the go-go times. By the decade's midpoint, we were one of the largest real estate developers in the country. In an average year, we handled about $1 billion in new construction. In 1989, we opened at least one new hotel every week.

Then the bottom dropped out of the U.S. real estate market in the fall of 1990. That crash—together with a general economic recession, the outbreak of the Persian Gulf War early in 1991, and other factors— effectively smacked us upside the head and left us reeling. We had plenty of good company; lots of businesses found themselves in trouble when the economy stumbled. But we got caught in the middle of our most ambitious expansion program to date.

To pull ourselves back from the brink, we had to take a number of austere measures. One of the most painful was letting most of our hotel development and architecture and construction departments go. With real estate dead in the water and a backlog of hotels to sell, we didn't need—and couldn't afford—to keep idle staff on the payroll.

Compared to other American companies that have "downsized," "right-sized," and otherwise reinvented themselves in the past ten years, Marriott's phased layoff of 1,000 employees out of more than 200,000 might not seem like a big deal. But for us, it was one of the roughest episodes we've been through. The cornerstone of our corporate culture has always been: "Take care of your employees, and they'll take care of your customers." Laying off a substantial number of people who had worked hard to contribute to our success felt like a betrayal of that philosophy.

On the surface, the layoff did look pretty bad. To outside observers, it probably appeared to be yet another nail in the coffin of already uneasy employee relations in 1990s American business. And, of course, for those who were being let go, the layoff didn't simply *look* bad, it *was* bad.

To the people inside Marriott who worked hard to make the experience as graceful and painless as possible, however, the downsizing was also a poignant opportunity to reaffirm our long-standing policy to "take care of" our employees.

Before I explain how we tried to do that, let me tell you about where the "employees-first" philosophy came from and why it's such a fundamental part of our corporate culture.

■

My father, J. Willard Marriott, was an extrovert. The second oldest in a family of eight children, he thrived on people. He was never happier than when engaged in lively conversation or a friendly debate.

Dad particularly enjoyed talking to his employees. Marriott's corporate legend is full of stories of my father perched comfortably on a hotel lobby sofa, listening to the family problems of one of our associates while senior managers cooled their heels waiting for him to return to the office.

I can confirm that the stories are true. Dad felt very strongly that the concerns and problems of the people who worked for him were always worth listening to. In his eyes, a successful company puts its employees first.

I couldn't agree more. When employees know that their problems will be taken seriously, that their ideas and insights matter, they're more comfortable and confident. In turn, they're better equipped to deliver their best on the job and to the customer. Everyone wins: the company, the employee, the customer.

The philosophy of putting employees first is particularly important in our industry, because Marriott is in the *people* business, not just the service business.

What do I mean by that? When your job is to supply customers with answers to two of life's basic needs—food and lodging—you're touching on pretty special human territory. Even if our customers aren't conscious of it, they have very definite expectations about not only the *tangible* parts of eating and sleeping— good food, a comfortable bed—but also the *intangibles* of those experiences: how they're greeted, how their questions are answered, how their special problems are handled. That's where the right human touch can make all the difference between a mediocre or poor experience and a positive, even unforgettable one.

Naturally, if the people who are responsible for supplying that human touch are unhappy, tired, stressed out, poorly trained, dissatisfied, or otherwise distracted, they're probably not going to do a good job. Their problems at home or behind the scenes will show in their work . . . and have a direct impact on guests' experiences.

On the flip side, if employees are content, confident, and generally happy with themselves and the job, their positive attitude will be felt in everything they do.

We have countless associates who have demonstrated remarkable personal generosity and kindness toward guests over the years. Stuff that no SOP can cover. If those associates didn't feel terrific about themselves, I don't think they would be able to do some of the things they've done. Some have loaned money out of their own pockets to guests who forgot their wallets. Others have played emergency babysitter, ordered (and picked up) replacement contact lenses, and put their weekend mechanic skills to work on conked-out cars. I've heard of associates lending shoes, jewelry, coats, blouses, and other items to guests who didn't pack them. One of the best stories I've come across involves an associate who loaned a nervous guest an entire suit of clothing for a critical job interview.

When you have employees who are willing, literally, to give a guest the clothes off their backs, doesn't taking good care of those employees make sense? Yet like developing and perfecting systems and SOPs, the concept of making employees feel really good about themselves seems to be missing from many companies' philosophies. Think of the number of heavily unionized industries that would be more productive and less tension-ridden if member companies had worked harder to take care of their employees from the beginning. Or how much more competitive American companies could be if relations between management and labor didn't require a continuous courting ritual to sort out respective interests?

Don't get me wrong. I'm not about to claim that every Marriott associate has at all times been treated with unfailing fairness and unflagging support. Of course not. No human institution handles human problems perfectly every time. But I do think that we are well above average, thanks to the emphasis we've always placed on the idea that we're all part of a team and that team members take care of one other.

A favorite story of mine—one that exemplifies this attitude—involves two Marriott associates who took it upon themselves to look after a third who was dying of cancer. For more than two years, the pair dropped by the woman's apartment or hospital bed on a daily basis. On one of my visits to the area, I stopped by to say hello to the ill woman. Both of her ministering angels were by her bedside. When she died about a year later, I had the honor of presenting the company's President's Award for extraordinary service to the two women who had shown such compassion for and devotion to their colleague.

But illness isn't the only time Marriott associates help each other out. Sometimes the assistance is as simple as covering for each other on the job to make sure everyone gets time off to attend special events and enjoy the holidays. Sometimes it's more dramatic. I know of truckloads of food, clothing, and necessities being collected, boxed up, and driven thousands of miles to people in need in the aftermath of hurricanes, floods, fires, earthquakes, and other natural disasters. Such generosity isn't unique to Marriott, of course, but it's a terrific sign of how far our concept of team-work goes.

Saying "employees first" is one thing, but making it

a permanent feature of your corporate culture requires *action*, not just words. I'd like to think that we put our money where our mouth is.

Training, for example, has been a core activity at Marriott since the early Hot Shoppes. Every day, hundreds of our associates new and old file into classrooms and kitchens around the globe to upgrade their skills. From cooking, computers, and communications to teamwork, time management, and TQM—you name it, we've probably taught it. In our early days, all of our managers and executives were trained to flip hamburgers, assemble salads, and make sundaes by longtime associates who were experts at the job. And if the manager didn't pass the associate's exacting standards, he did not "graduate" until he improved. Period. No excuses. For many years we sent our chief financial officer and other nonoperations executives through the company's "food school" to gain a bit of hands-on experience with the products and services that form the basis of Marriott's world.

Our emphasis on training of all kinds and at all levels is partly a reflection of the aspects of our corporate culture that you've read about in earlier chapters: hands-on management and attention to detail. But it's also a recognition that we can hardly expect our associates to do their jobs *well* if we haven't shown them *how*. They deserve to know that the organization is willing to invest in building their skills and knowledge to give them more confidence on the job, as well as a chance to keep moving up the ladder. It's central to our employees-first philosophy to give them both the opportunities and the tools to succeed.

One of our most recent employee initiatives is Pathways to Independence, a welfare-to-work program developed by our human resources department to train low- or no-skilled workers for jobs with the company. During a six-week, no-pay internship, former welfare recipients are taught basic work skills that qualify them to hold hourly positions. For many, this is the first opportunity they've had to master skills that most of us take for granted. Not everyone who applies makes it into the Pathways program; only 25 percent of those interviewed for the program are accepted. And not everyone sticks with it, in spite of yeoman labor on the part of our trainers to help trainees overcome self-esteem problems, family troubles, and other challenges. Pathways hasn't been without its frustrations and issues, but we hope it becomes a model for other businesses.

Given our penchant for systems, you probably won't be surprised to learn that we're big on providing safety nets for our associates. By safety nets, I mean the kinds of support systems that let employees know that they're not out there on the job alone, with no one to turn to for help if they need it. Some call it "overmanaging by design." We just think it's a natural outgrowth of our hands-on management philosophy and our drive to get the details right.

Our overall systems and our training programs, of course, provide part of the safety net, but there are other aspects as well. A good example is the process we use when we open a new hotel. Weeks ahead of time, a special team composed of veterans from other Marriott hotels takes up residence at the property to help the new staff debug systems, put on the finishing touches, and roll out the red carpet on opening day. A skeleton crew sticks around afterward to help out until they're not needed anymore. All that fuss might seem like overkill, but I've yet to hear of a GM of a new property who wasn't grateful for the support.

Another area in which we've invested considerable energy and attention in providing support systems is our work-life programs. Marriott is hardly the only major company in America to recognize the increasing complexity of employees' lives, but I'd like to think we're at the forefront of doing good things to help our associates cope. This is an area where we clearly have an opportunity to demonstrate the employees-first philosophy.

One of the biggest employer challenges for Marriott has always been in helping our associates juggle family responsibilities with duties on the job. The task has become even more daunting as the nation's hourly workforce has become more multicultural in makeup. Once upon a time we had perhaps at most a dozen foreign languages spoken among our employees; we now have more than eighty. Many of our hourly associates must cope with complicated immigration procedures, interpersonal cultural clashes, and social discrimination, in addition to the pressures of child care, elder care, substance or domestic abuse, or housing problems.

What toll do these problems take on our associates and, by extension, on the company as a whole? Well, as I said earlier, if you have employees who aren't feeling terribly good about themselves, they're not likely to give their best on the job. An associate who must scramble to replace a baby-sitter who canceled or who's worried sick about a recent call she received from an immigration lawyer isn't going to be in the best shape to deliver that all-important "human touch." What that troubled associate needs is a bit of the human touch herself, in the form of understanding and assistance.

In many cases, our associates help each other out. But for those times when colleagues and bosses aren't the answer, there are alternative sources of support. One option is a toll-free consultation service for our lodging associates staffed by social workers who field questions and find solutions to just about any problem. And they can do it in more than 100 languages.

We rolled out the 800 Associate Resource Line (ARL) on a national basis in 1996, after a two-year regional trial run. Although the program is based on intensive studies of our associates' needs, the thinking behind it is actually pretty simple. At heart, it's really just a slightly higher-tech version of my father's "let's-sit-on-the-sofa-and-talk-this-out" approach to taking care of employees. An associate with any kind of question, problem, or crisis can dial up the ARL and immediately connect with a trained professional who listens, counsels, and follows through until a solution is found.

In addition to providing concrete help, the program gives our associates a sign of our commitment to them. The vast majority who have tapped into the ARL felt even more positive about working at Marriott after getting help with their problems. That's particularly important to me. I want our associates to think of the company as more than a clock in–clock out job.

Marriott, naturally, benefits when the ARL is able to lend a hand to an associate. We wouldn't be able to justify the program if it didn't. But more important, we've seen dramatic drops in turnover, absenteeism, tardiness, and short workdays among those using the service, all of which are very good signs that those associates feel more in control of their lives. That's what it's all about.

Helping associates feel in control of their fates is also one of the engines behind the company's profit sharing program, which has been in place since 1959. I'm sure I don't have to explain the philosophy of profit sharing, and I certainly won't bore you with the mechanics. Suffice it to say that we think profit sharing is a fitting reflection of our corporate culture's emphasis on teamwork. We've had scores of longtime associates retire with hefty nest eggs because they stuck with us twenty, thirty, forty years or more. Those associates took care of Marriott for many years, and we, in turn, paid them back.

Another long-term tradition at Marriott that falls under the employees-first umbrella is promotion from within. To use just one year as an example, in 1983 about one-third of all new Marriott managers were promoted from hourly ranks. One former Marriott executive told me recently that he thinks the "genius" of our company lies in treating all of our associates as if they were managers. I'm not sure I'd go quite that far—every organization needs leaders *and* followers—but I think he's on the right track. We've always been more impressed by hard work and dedication than paper credentials. And we always will be.

Another long-standing practice that I have no intention of giving up is my own habit of answering nearly all of the letters that come into my office from Marriott associates. If an employee takes the time to write me, he or she is owed a response. Usually, associates contact my office because they've got a problem or complaint that they want to bring to my attention. Small or large, the matter is investigated and we get back to them. Some of what's driving me is—you guessed it—my hands-on habit, but it's also because I want to be sure that every Marriott employee feels that he or she can get a fair hearing. Even if the problem isn't resolved in the associate's favor, I'd at least like him to know that he received respectful attention.

All of the above are important—training, work-life programs, safety nets, profit sharing, promotion, a willingness to investigate concerns—but none is as important as having *hands-on managers* in place who possess the people skills to support, encourage, lead, inspire, and listen to associates. A manager without those skills is going against the grain of the organization and seventy years of corporate culture. He or she might be able to make good financial results for a short time, but in the end, the lack of people skills will always catch up.

Let me give you an example. A couple of years ago, on a property tour, I noticed that the new general manager of one of our hotels was making impressive numbers in his first nine months on the job, but the associates at the property seemed to me to be unusually subdued. Even the folks at the front desk—roles almost always filled by extroverts—looked uneasy.

Curious to get a glimpse of the associates at work when the boss wasn't around, I made a point of getting away from the GM for a short stroll of my own. I soon saw and heard enough to convince me that the whole staff was walking on eggshells. Closer investigation revealed that the associates were scared of the GM: he was bullying, punitive, and unsympathetic to their concerns.

In spite of his good numbers, the manager was *not* good for the health of the associates. He didn't embrace our employees-first philosophy. The solution was clear: we had to let him go.

Speaking of letting people go, let me get back to the story about Marriott's layoff.

When trouble hit us in the fall of 1990, we had to retrench pretty quickly. One of the most wrenching decisions we made was to effectively eliminate our huge hotel development and architecture and construction (A&C) departments. We had been developing about 100 new hotels a year in the latter half of the 1980s. A&C had grown into a gigantic assembly-line operation. There truly was nothing comparable in the American hotel industry . . . or most other industries, for that matter.

Almost overnight, we had to close down the assembly line. Marriott had never in its sixty-three-year history faced the prospect of letting go two entire departments. Growth had always been our motto; we were accustomed to *hiring*, not *firing*. But we had no choice. We couldn't pretend that there was going to be new building when most of the hotels in Marriott's pipeline had been halted or scrapped.

The only thing we could do was handle the layoff in a way that would take as much of the sting out of it as possible, for all parties—both those who were to depart and those who would stay behind.

I intentionally emphasize the fact that we had *two* "audiences" to take care of during the phasing-down process. It was important to us to do our best to help *all* of our associates cope with anxiety about the future. The people who were leaving deserved our support in finding other work, if possible, and the folks who stayed on needed to be reassured that their hard work was appreciated and they needn't waste energy agonizing over whether they, too, would soon lose their jobs.

Novices to downsizing, we had the remarkable luck

to stumble upon a terrific consultant who helped us with every aspect of setting up an off-site outplacement center near our corporate headquarters. The team responsible for handling the outplacement effort spent hours working out every possible option to help people prepare résumés, conduct job searches, and deal with the stress of facing an extraordinarily tight employment market. At our center, departing associates had access to professional counseling, interview coaching, and a bank of cubicles equipped with telephones where they could come each day to pursue job leads.

When the layoffs were announced, we braced ourselves. Not surprisingly, the anger of being laid off often translates into litigation, and we had been warned that despite our efforts to provide for our employees, we weren't going to be immune.

The concern turned out to be groundless. Out of more than 1,000 people, only 2 took legal action against us, and those claims were minor and amicably resolved. In fact, I was touched when a number of departing employees took the trouble to thank us for our outplacement help. I was likewise pleased that we ultimately were able to place more than 90 percent of those looking for jobs.

There's no way to prove it, but I believe the fact that the employees who had to leave us had enjoyed a good tenure at Marriott—had been, in effect, well taken care of—is what made the difference. Had those associates felt they had been treated carelessly during their years with us, I doubt we would have seen such understanding on their part. When put to the toughest test possible, Marriott's employees-first philosophy more than lived up to the ideal my father intended when he put it into place seventy years ago. As you might well imagine, we have no intention of changing it!

4

HE WHO LISTENS WELL LEARNS WELL

It takes two to speak the truth—
one to speak, and another to hear.

—HENRY DAVID THOREAU

Many years ago, a group of Marriott executives was waiting in our boardroom to update me on a hotel project I was particularly excited about. Senior-level representatives from all the key functions were there: feasibility, finance, design, construction, operations, etc. The group apparently killed time by talking about what an absolutely terrible idea the project was.

A few minutes later, I walked in the door, clapped my hands together enthusiastically, and asked, "So, how's my project looking?" Everybody responded, "Well, Bill, it's looking good, really good." Everybody except one fellow, a junior executive who had not opened his mouth.

Turning to him, I commented: "You haven't said anything. What do *you* think?"

He proceeded to rattle off all the reasons why the project was a disaster in the making—the same reasons that everyone around the table had been airing just minutes before I came in.

I paused a moment and then replied: "You know, you're absolutely right. Kill it."

I walked out. Jaws dropped around the table and that was the end of the project.

■

I tell this Marriott version of *The Emperor's New Clothes* to make two points: One, most people will do anything to avoid being the bearer of bad news, and two, thank goodness there are a hardy few who *won't*. The episode was also an excellent reminder that I needed to keep working on my listening skills.

After more than forty years in business, I've concluded that listening is the single most important on-the-job skill that a good manager can cultivate. A leader who doesn't listen well risks missing critical information, losing (or never winning) the confidence of staff and peers, and forfeiting the opportunity to be a proactive, hands-on manager.

I'm convinced that there are few natural-born good listeners. Somewhere along the way, good listeners *learned* to be good listeners. I suspect they discovered that there are rewards for keeping your ears open.

One key to effective listening lies in recognizing what *kind* of listening works best in different situations. For example, sometimes good listening simply requires keeping your mouth closed. Whenever I make this point, I think of a prescription a pundit once suggested: "To say the right thing at the right time, keep still most of the time."

Keeping still isn't always easy. In fact, it can be torture to hold your tongue and let someone else talk, especially if the talker is slow about getting to the point. Still, it's a vital skill to learn. So is mastering the body language that shows that you're interested in what's being said. Keeping quiet won't get you very far if the speaker can see by the glazed look in your eyes or impatient tapping of a pencil that you'd rather be somewhere else.

In working on my own listening skills, I've found it useful to watch and adopt the body language of people whose listening skills I admire, people whom I enjoy talking to precisely because they listen to me so well. Folks like that have a knack for making you feel like you're the only person in the world they want to talk to at that particular moment. Sometimes, simply by mimicking their alert posture and eye contact, you'll find yourself slipping into being genuinely interested in a conversation you thought you were too tired or impatient to pay attention to. Better yet, you soon learn that you don't have to act the part. You've reaped enough benefits from keeping still that you do it automatically.

When you open your ears, open your mind, too. Listening should be an opportunity to learn. You won't learn much if you make up your mind before you've had a chance to hear anything. In my case—as I found out in that revealing boardroom session—it's especially important not to signal that I've come to my own conclusions too early in a meeting. The less I say, the less I sway the discussion. I'd rather have people feel comfortable suggesting wild-eyed arguments or pie-in-the-sky concepts than take the chance that someone is holding back a good idea because they're picking up signals that I've already come to a decision. I especially want people to feel comfortable about raising red flags. If ever I need to be reminded of this point, all I have to do is think about how much money might have been wasted on a bad idea if that young executive had not spoken his mind that day.

Another former Marriott executive—now a CEO

himself—said recently that one of the things he most appreciated about working at Marriott was the fact that he could promote and try to win support for his ideas up to the very end, the final vote. No one cut him off or shut him out before he'd had his chance to make his best case, no matter how off the wall the idea.

I've also found it's a good idea to be conscious of subtle, potentially negative signals that your listening habits might be sending out. Managers in particular need to be alert to how they divvy up their listening time. Occasionally, I've heard the criticism that I listen to too many people and seem to give equal weight to what each has to say, regardless of how knowledgeable or senior they are.

Let me turn that criticism on its head. What kind of message would I be sending to the organization if I gave an hour to finance, but only ten hurried minutes to human resources? Or if I never gave anyone under the senior vice presidential level more than thirty seconds of my time? I'd rather err on the side of hearing more than I might need to make a good decision and in the process keep all the troops in the loop.

Along those same lines, I believe strongly in the practice of listening to the organization's heartbeat myself, instead of relying exclusively on my direct reports and senior staff for information. I make a habit of calling directly into our various divisions and levels to hear straight talk from associates. In part, this is simply a reflection of being a hands-on manager, but it's also due to the fact that I think the organization benefits from knowing that I'm accessible to more than my senior staff. And I benefit from having multiple points of contact in the organization.

Sometimes good listening means *not* keeping still. It calls for action, to combat the natural tendency of staff to avoid telling the boss bad news or rocking the boat. This more active version of listening requires asking questions in order to break through someone's hesitancy and get to the heart of a problem. It's a particularly important skill for high-level leaders (presidents, CEOs) who, by their lofty positions, often intimidate junior staff. I'm a great believer in the phrase, "What do you think?" It works wonders.

On a recent visit to a hotel managed by one of our franchisees, I noticed that guest scores on the attitude of the dining room hostess were below Marriott's standard. I asked the manager what he thought the problem was, and he said he wasn't sure. But I could tell by his uneasy body language that there was more to the story.

Then I asked what the hostess's pay was. When he told me, I realized she was being paid at least $2 per hour less than market rate. The manager proceeded to explain that headquarters needed to okay her increase and that he was reluctant to ask.

In a thirty-second conversation, I had discovered three serious problems. One, the home office was exerting too much control; the manager should have been able to raise the hostess's wages to market level without seeking permission. Two, senior management was obviously placing more emphasis on profits than on customer satisfaction. Three, the fact that the manager was *afraid* even to ask about a raise suggested that the attitude of senior management was not a friendly one. In essence, his superiors had shown themselves to be inferior listeners.

All three problems were solved in short order, and soon the hostess's score on guest satisfaction climbed to where it should have been in the first place. All it took was breaking through the manager's reticence and showing him that someone was willing to hear him out—something his senior managers had apparently signaled they were not willing to do.

Listening certainly should not be limited to the heart of the house. At Marriott, we count on our guests to tell us what we're doing right and wrong. It's the only way we can know for sure whether we're giving them what they want. Over the years, our guests have suggested many incidentals and small touches. Today, most of our guest rooms have irons, ironing boards, blow-dryers, brighter lightbulbs, hand cream, and one item that our female guests uniformly clamored for: hangers with skirt-friendly clips.

One of our newest innovations—The Room That Works—grew out of a listening-to-the-customer exercise. A couple of years ago, we set out to design a better guest room for business travelers. We pulled together some focus groups and quickly discovered that high on their wish list was a change in the placement of electrical outlets in our rooms. Guests wanted them to be visible and accessible.

At first glance, the request seemed odd. After all, for more than thirty years, our interior designers had gone out of their way to *hide* electrical outlets. Holes in the wall weren't exactly considered an attractive design element.

That was fine in the days before laptop computers. Today, business travelers bring their laptops with them and want to be able to plug in quickly and easily to work on documents, check e-mail, etc. They were sick and tired of crawling around under desks and moving furniture to find a free outlet.

If we had not asked the question and been willing to listen to the answer, we might never have known how much this one simple change meant to the comfort of our business guests.

Valuable as they are, focus groups are not the only

time or place for listening to customers. Part of the attention to detail and bias for action that Marriott's associates strive for includes picking up on a guest's needs or desires—even anticipating them, if possible.

During a stay at a Marriott hotel a few years ago, one of our senior executives came down to the dining room one morning and ordered a bowl of cereal with fresh fruit for breakfast. He selected strawberries from the menu choices. The waitress, who had no idea who her customer was, delivered the bad news that there were no strawberries to be had that day. Would he like a sliced banana instead? she asked. He hesitated, said okay, and went back to reading his newspaper.

A few minutes later, the waitress materialized with his bowl of cereal, complete with bananas *and* strawberries on the side. She had found strawberries in the kitchen after all, and, since he had sounded unsure about settling for a banana, she'd brought him some of each so he could choose or enjoy both as he wished.

He beamed as she walked away. Thanks to that single, simple gesture of listening to the customer's uncertainty, the waitress got that guest's day off to a terrific start.

Unfortunately, not everyone listens as well as that waitress did. I can think of at least one longtime executive who gained a reputation for being a poor listener toward the end of his career with Marriott. He never liked anything that anybody had to say. If someone offered a new idea, he would shoot it down with the same repetitive set of reasons. Too much money, waste of time, too risky, whatever. Soon, no one wanted to tell him anything, because they knew what his response would be. He lost his credibility as a listener and, as a result, found himself cut out of substantive discussions and decisions. He forfeited the support of his people and finally lost his job.

Selective listening is almost as bad as not listening at all. You don't do yourself—or anyone else—any favors when you filter out bad news. We learned that lesson the hard way at the end of the 1980s when we chose to downplay signals that the hotel industry was on the verge of being seriously overbuilt. We wanted so much to believe in our own invincibility that we focused only on positive news and turned a deaf ear to anything that we didn't want to hear. The price for that kind of half-listening was high.

Our "it-won't-happen-to-us" attitude was exacerbated by the persuasiveness of one executive whose reassuring eloquence overcame my gut feeling that the company ought to have exercised more caution. His arguments for continuing to build hotels in spite of signs of recession were so smooth, so reasonable, so apparently logical that I let myself believe everything would be fine. What I learned, of course, was that just because someone is a polished speaker or presenter doesn't mean that his or her ideas are always right. Conversely, someone who is a bit shy or awkward about speaking up might well be worth listening to. For me, the episode provided an excellent if unwelcome lesson in not judging the *substance* of a message by the appealing *style* of its delivery.

Ultimately, even the most skilled listening has limits. At some point, debate and fact gathering must come to an end. A decision must be made based upon what's been learned. This is the juncture at which the true mettle of an organization's overall listening skills is put to the test. If the environment for discussion has been an open one in which people know that their ideas, insights, and concerns are treated with respect, the result will be well-informed choices. Not every decision will be perfect, of course, but when a decision does turn out to be wrong, there will be comfort in knowing that it *wasn't* wrong because someone forgot to ask the $64,000 question: "What do *you* think?"

5

PRESERVE ORDER AMID CHANGE

> The art of progress is to preserve order amid change
> and to preserve change amid order.
>
> —ALFRED NORTH WHITEHEAD

Building a business can be boring.

Heresy? Ask anyone who has been at the top of a company for more than a few years. The daily grind of business consists largely of taking care of thousands of tiny, laborious details. Very little of what a company does ever sees the light of day, much less the camera lights of press conferences, photo shoots, or commercials.

Why begin a chapter about *growth* with an unappetizing image of *hard work*?

No grunt work = no growth. No growth = no future.

Let me give you an example of the kind of no-frills work that comes with my job. Each month I join a team of Marriott executives in reviewing "red" and "yellow" hotels that are experiencing guest-service problems. The idea is to figure out how to—you guessed it—move them back into the all-systems-go "green" category.

Is this glamorous work? No. In terms of fun, does it outrank a gala opening party for a new resort? Definitely not. Is it necessary? You bet. We can't expect to add new hotels to our system successfully if we don't take care of the ones we already have.

The kind of nitty-gritty work I just described is vital to the growth of our lodging business. It's also a reflection of another kind of growth that is equally important to our health and well-being: the growth of Marriott as an *organization*.

In the past few years, the topic of "growing" a business organization has been a hot one. In spite of the wave of attention, when companies talk about growth, they are still generally referring to the process of adding units, increasing sales, improving margins, and bolstering stock prices. We're no exception. We've always been driven to make our numbers.

Between 1927 and 1957, when we opened our first hotel, Marriott's financial picture grew from the original $6,000 that my father and his partner, Hugh Colton, borrowed and pooled to more than $36 million in annual sales. The only year that didn't bring an increase in earnings was 1942, a war year. After we entered the lodging business in 1957, growth continued at a rewarding pace. We hit $1 billion in annual sales in our fiftieth anniversary year, 1977. Just before we encountered the problems of 1990, we enjoyed an unbroken string of a dozen years in which annual growth hovered around 20 percent.

Twenty percent, in fact, became a magic number for us. We began using the shorthand 20/20 to sum up our annual growth goal: 20 percent growth in sales and 20 percent return on equity. Among other things, the catchy phrase gave our large, far-flung organization an easy-to-remember mission. One former Marriott executive—now at the helm of another major company— was always impressed that our frontline employees, located thousands of miles from corporate headquarters, could reply "20/20" when asked what their goal was for the year. He tells me that his new organization has no comparable battle cry.

I was particularly pleased to hear that our 20/20 mission spread so readily to the field. Like our monthly red-yellow-green hotel review sessions, it tells me that Marriott has succeeded in putting into place key organizational mechanisms that support and sustain the growth of our businesses. Even as we've been hammering away at making our numbers, we've been growing our organization.

When you cut to the chase of what growth in all its dimensions is all about, I think the quote I selected to kick off this chapter sums it up well: "The art of progress is to preserve order amid change and to preserve change amid order."

For businesses, this translates into: To grow successfully, you must *stay true* to who you are, even while working feverishly to *change* who you are.

Businesses that hope to be around for the long haul need to find a balance between these two inherently conflicting processes. The ability to maintain order *and* embrace change simultaneously is no small feat. It's a little like ballet. Executed well, it looks effortless. Only when there's a misstep does it become clear that something's out of kilter.

Back in the late 1950s, one of our competitors in the lodging industry broke out of the gate fast and furiously with a terrific new product. The interstate highway system was just beginning to boom, and the company moved quickly to take advantage of the new travel market. When it came to saturating the landscape, the chain displayed a positive, go-go growth mentality and a knack for picking locations. But the company soon discovered that its internal structure wasn't sufficiently developed to handle the avalanche of growth. The organization was not able to find the critical balance between order and change. Without strong organizational systems to manage and adapt to fast-paced growth, the company tripped, lost its early lead to competitors, and never completely recovered.

Our initial experience with hotel franchising in the 1960s was a similar case of order-change imbalance. In 1968, we announced that we would begin franchising Marriott hotels on a limited basis. The fact that we were franchising at all was itself a major change for Marriott's "order." As I mentioned in an earlier chapter, my father heartily disliked franchising, because he didn't like the idea of not having day-to-day hands-on control over the management of his business.

For a company that is as systems-oriented as we are, we really fell down on developing the systems we needed to make our initial foray into franchising work. First, we jumped in too fast and had to beat a hasty retreat when we found that we had far too many unqualified applicants trying to give us a check in exchange for a Marriott franchise.

No sooner did we get a handle on the application process and narrow the field than we inadvertently tripped ourselves up by deciding that the franchised Marriott hotels—to be called Marriott Inns—would be specially designed to distinguish them from the company's own hotels. From today's standpoint, the decision is a strange one; one of the strengths of franchising is to have all properties appear to be part of one seamless system. Our choice also flies in the face of one of our most cherished goals: consistency.

The long and the short of it is that we soon backtracked a bit along what had been proudly touted as a new avenue of growth for Marriott. We scaled back our ambitions, opened fewer franchised hotels, and, in general, moved far more slowly than originally planned.

On the surface, it might appear that the problem stemmed from a lack of organizational capability. But I don't think know-how was the real issue. The management systems of Marriott's "order" are so strong that we'd have found the right answers and gotten ourselves well-organized before too long. After all, franchising was new to us, but running hotels was not. The real problem was one of mind-set. As an organization, we simply didn't embrace franchising as wholeheartedly as we needed to make it a success. Even as we jumped into "change" enthusiastically, a key component of our "order" resisted adapting to and supporting the change. The very fact that we didn't want to risk having the franchised hotels be confused with "real" Marriott hotels by looking too much alike probably says it all.

Today, we've thoroughly embraced hotel franchising. It's one of our major growth platforms. In fact, the number of franchised hotels under our various flags now exceeds the number of hotels owned or managed by Marriott itself. Some of the change has to do with the fact that we now have products in the Marriott family of brands that lend themselves to franchising. But the most important shift has been in our attitude. Once we decided to think of ourselves as a franchiser—as a franchise *organization*—the rest fell into place.

Our experience with franchising wasn't limited to the lodging side of the business. We gave it a try on the restaurant side, too, with our Roy Rogers and Big Boy chains. We acquired Big Boy in 1967 and Roy Rogers (originally Robee's) in 1968. I won't go into the details of the acquisitions, but both purchases took us into the unfamiliar territory of restaurant franchising. We stayed with the businesses for the better part of twenty years, but we frankly did not embrace franchising any more fervently on the food side of the business than we did in lodging. In part, we were hampered by certain provisions in the original Big Boy purchase agreements. But mainly, it was another instance of not being ready to think of ourselves as a committed franchiser. The result was that we really didn't grow the businesses as aggressively as someone else might have. We got out of both in the late 1980s.

One of the biggest changes to have an impact on our growth both as an organization and as a business occurred in the late 1970s when we overhauled our corporate financing philosophy. This one modification alone has reverberated throughout the company for the last two decades.

For the first fifty years of our existence, we had what could be called a "bean-counter" mentality toward finance. Property leases and traditional mortgages were pretty much the extent of our financial universe.

As long as we were leasing and building small facilities like restaurants, our simple financing approach worked very well. But by the mid-1970s, when we were trying to move into the big leagues, the formula was holding us back. We were especially hampered on the lodging side of the business, where the price tag for a single full-service convention hotel could easily run into the tens of millions of dollars. Huge mortgages not only limited the number of hotels we could build, but put a real strain on what we could show in the way of returns to our shareholders.

Beginning in 1978, with the help of a couple of very talented financial minds—Gary Wilson and Al Checchi (now major stakeholders in Northwest Airlines, among other things)—Marriott revolutionized its entire approach to the lodging business. The most important element of the change in the philosophy is one I mentioned earlier: our decision not to be a hotel ownership company, but to focus instead on being a hotel *management* company.

The most visible impact of the decision was seen on the company balance sheet almost immediately. We began by selling to investors several of the hotels that we had built before 1978. As part of the deals, we signed long-term management contracts and kept a significant part of the cash flow from the properties. No longer held down by heavy mortgages, we gained more flexibility.

The next revolutionary change took the form of turning ourselves into a major real estate developer, but with a firm commitment not to retain the real estate. Why wait around for others to build hotels and ask us to manage them when we could construct them, sell them, and keep long-term management contracts? Why wait to be invited to the dance when we could build the ballroom and hire the orchestra ourselves?

Marriott's order responded to the call for development capacity by setting up a huge construction pipeline. The company had long had an architecture and construction team, but the scale of building was going to be bigger than anything we'd ever done in the past. Feeding the pipeline would also require much more complex financing resources than Marriott had been accustomed to dealing with.

Creative financing ideas soon bounced around our boardroom, helped along by major changes in the federal tax code in 1981 that fueled real estate development. To grow as planned, we had to transform ourselves into a deal-savvy organization. Once again, the order adapted. We found ourselves easing into the let's-make-a-deal mind-set that characterized much of 1980s business. Our legal department quickly mastered the intricacies of syndications, limited partnerships, and other real estate investment vehicles.

Deal-making meant debt. My father had always viewed debt as an evil to be avoided at all costs. He had lived through the Great Depression and never shook his fear of borrowing money. But to achieve the magnitude of growth that would move Marriott to the next level, debt financing was vital. I talked, he listened; he grimaced, I borrowed. The order adjusted yet again to fit our new needs.

The three D's I've just described—development, deals, and debt—came as a package and brought fundamental, institution-wide change to Marriott's order in the 1980s. The organization largely dealt well with the growing pains that came with change (we eventually sold more than $6 billion in hotels in the 1980s), but not without a bit of stumbling toward the end of the day.

One of the most worrisome aspects of the kind of sweeping institutional change and growth I've talked about above has been its potential for endangering a key aspect of our order: our corporate culture. Our evolution from a handful of local restaurants into a huge multifaceted, global enterprise has made the care and feeding of our original culture a tremendous challenge. We've been determined not to lose the essential qualities and priorities that have defined Marriott as an organization from the very beginning.

One of our most crucial tasks is to try to maintain a family feeling in a company that now has 225,000 employees. Size alone makes it a challenge to communicate effectively with associates working at hundreds of locations around the world. Like other large companies, we also must grapple with rapid employee turnover and the negative effects of social forces that seem to fracture lives more readily than ever.

If I had to pick one facet of our corporate order that I maintain is absolutely vital to our future well-being, it would be hands-on management. In the fight to preserve the family atmosphere at Marriott, it's probably our best weapon. Every increase in the number of properties in our system means that my own visits to individual sites will be spaced farther apart, making it more difficult for me to be visible as often as I'd like. The organization will be more dependent than ever on hands-on managers in the field who can carry on the tradition that my dad started and that I've tried to continue.

Another challenge that organizational growth presents to our corporate values is in the area of quality control. Rapid changes in size and scope can cause a company to lose command of its processes and products. On this score, our long history of systems and SOPs, plus our huge internal training program, will ensure success. That doesn't mean that change won't figure in the picture; our programs will continue to evolve to stay in step with guests' and associates' needs. *How* we achieve consistency might change, but the drive for consistency itself won't.

The third point of our corporate culture—taking care of our associates—will also continue to be a top priority for us. Like hands-on management, it's a key factor in maintaining the company's family spirit. The programs and attitudes that I talked about earlier aren't apt to change anytime soon. They more likely will grow over time. In fact, a large part of the order of Marriott is and will continue to be devoted specifically to counterbalancing negative change that we think would ruin the good thing we've got going.

Underlying these challenges is something we should

never lose sight of, no matter how large or prosperous the company becomes: our core values. One episode brought this point home to me in a way I'll never forget.

My father was a devoted fan of AstroTurf. He loved the fresh green color and the texture and wanted us to use it every chance we could, to cover bare concrete sidewalks, swimming pool decks, room balconies, and virtually anything else that didn't move. Dad was constantly after me to use large quantities. He even checked AstroTurf prices on a near-weekly basis at the country hardware store not far from the family farm in Virginia. He would walk into the office on Monday morning, quote the latest price, and wait expectantly for me to jump at the chance to buy in bulk at the store's low rate, which was about half our procurement price. If we bought it in the country, he pointed out, we could use twice as much.

The AstroTurf update became a predictable part of our weekly ritual. But it wasn't until May 1982 that I really appreciated its true significance. That month, I was confronted with the task of making the biggest financial decision of my career. For several months, we had been working feverishly to finalize development plans for a new hotel in Times Square at Broadway and 45th Street in New York City. I had to decide whether to commit Marriott to build a $500 million hotel in a run-down, seedy area that might or might not come back to life. It was a huge risk.

On the afternoon of the final day that we had to make up our minds, I was in my office mulling over last-minute details of the deal. The phone rang. The landowner in New York City was calling to remind me that this was the last day of our option. If we didn't buy the land by the end of the day, the price would go up. Before I could take his call, another telephone line lit up. This one was the general contractor reporting that he could not get a "no-strike" clause accepted in the construction contract. Did we want to take a strike risk? Just then another light on my telephone lit up. The New York City mayor's office was calling to get confirmation of our decision to go forward (they hoped) so the project could be announced at a big press conference. Last, but not least, the fourth light came on. My father was on the line. My secretary wanted to know whom I wanted to talk to first.

I took my father's call. In an angry voice, he demanded: "When are you going to put AstroTurf on the balconies of the Twin Bridges hotel?"

Just when you might think I would have been most dismayed to have to listen to yet another lecture on the merits of AstroTurf, I was in fact relieved. My father's simple, down-to-earth question about fake grass had the effect of bringing *me* down to earth, too, reminding me of the company's real priorities: attention to detail and looking after our customers' comfort. A new $500 million hotel wasn't going to mean much if in the process of building it we left behind the fundamental values that had helped us become successful enough to be *able* to build it.

Our decision about whether or not to build the hotel? The 1,900-room Marriott Marquis opened on Times Square in 1985. But not before I made sure that we had plenty of AstroTurf on hand. . . .

6
PRESERVE CHANGE AMID ORDER

If the shoe fits, you're not allowing for growth.

—ROBERT N. COONS

It is common sense to take a method and try it.
If it fails, admit it frankly and try another.
But above all, try something.

—FRANKLIN DELANO ROOSEVELT

In the last chapter, I talked mainly about the organizational challenges that Marriott has faced in transforming itself from a small company into a large one. Those growing pains reflected one half of Alfred North Whitehead's proverb about progress: the task of preserving order amid change. In this chapter, I'll focus on the other half of Whitehead's charge: the job of preserving change amid order.

Given the head-spinning speed of change nowadays,

there might not seem to be much to say about the need to *preserve* it. After all, aren't we awash in change? In the seventy years since Marriott opened its doors, the world has been altered almost beyond recognition. My parents went into business the day Charles Lindbergh began his legendary transatlantic solo flight—May 20, 1927. My mother, now in her nineties, has lived to see the sound barrier broken, men walk on the moon, and space shuttles orbit the globe. That's just a razor-thin slice of life in the realm of science; changes in politics and society have been revolutionary, too. And the pace of change just keeps getting faster.

Marriott, of course, has neither caused nor endured the kind of dramatic upheavals that make headlines and history books. On the other hand, we've evolved in our own way over the years. The majority of businesses that we're in today didn't exist in the company's portfolio twenty years ago.

A critical ingredient in our evolution has been a willingness to experiment. During the past seven decades, we've tried our hand at many new lines of business, always in search of fresh avenues for growth. Sometimes we've struck gold. Sometimes we've stumbled. Either way, we've tried to keep in mind one simple truth: Change is to business what oxygen is to life. In a word, vital.

Change can also be frightening and even paralyzing.

It brings with it the potential for error and embarrassment. One of the best lessons we've taken to heart over the years is that of not letting ourselves be crippled by mistakes. Instead, we've tried to learn something from them and move on.

This is where businesses can run into trouble in the preserving-change-amid-order area: allowing setbacks to make them too cautious, fearful, or just plain suspicious of experimentation and innovation. "Order" gets the upper hand, and before you know it, the only "change" being experienced is that of going out of business.

Change, naturally, is easier to take if you're the one initiating it. But in business—as in life—you're not always in control. Competitors can be coming at you from all sides, forcing you to run to stay ahead. Or you're the one going after somebody else who's gotten out in front of you.

Both of those scenarios have certainly been true for us. We've had another compelling impetus for change as well. As a public company, Marriott has had to be responsive to our shareholders. Our efforts to diversify and grow have been driven to an important (although not exclusive) degree by the need to show shareholders that we can produce results.

Actually, the company's earliest diversification came sixteen years before going public. The In-Flite airline catering division was launched in 1937 when my father noticed customers taking hot coffee and food "to go" from one of our Hot Shoppes near Washington's airport. During the next fifty years, we built the division from the original contract with Rickenbacker's Eastern Air Transport into a more than $1 billion business before selling it in 1989. Along the way, we grew In-Flite by building flight kitchens ourselves and acquiring a number of independently owned kitchens and small catering companies. One of the most important things that In-Flite did for us was diversify Marriott in international terms. Our first overseas operation was a flight kitchen in Caracas, Venezuela, acquired in 1966. At its height, In-Flite had kitchens in twenty countries.

The next diversification effort was more dramatic, because it took us beyond restaurants and catering. After nearly thirty years in the food business—Hot Shoppes, In-Flite airline catering, and food service management—Marriott launched into the lodging business with what we proudly dubbed the "world's largest motor hotel" in January 1957, four years after the company went public.

It would be nice to claim that our first major diversification as a public company was no accident. In truth, our Twin Bridges motor hotel was mostly a stroke of good luck.

The site for Twin Bridges (now torn down) was just south of Washington, D.C., on Route 1, close to National Airport, the Pentagon, a bridge across the Potomac River, and other major transportation arteries. The *location* we selected was not by chance; my father loved to put his Hot Shoppes at busy intersections and—when possible—near bridges. He reasoned that highways might be relocated, but bridges never move.

The groundwork for Twin Bridges was laid when my dad opened a Hot Shoppe on Route 1 at the entrance to the 14th Street Bridge in 1936. In 1950, he purchased a large piece of land just across the highway, with an eye toward building a new central office, food preparation facility, and warehouse for the Hot Shoppes. But our executive vice president Milt Barlow told Dad that he thought the site had great commercial potential. Why not build a big motel? he suggested. After all, 125,000 cars passed by the spot every day, the airport was close, the Pentagon was next door, and downtown Washington was only five minutes away. In short order, plans for a 365-room hotel were drawn up, and we entered the lodging business in 1957.

Success, of course, did not come immediately. In the 1950s, the hotel business tended to be seasonal: Twin Bridges would fill up with tourists in the spring and summer and empty out in the fall and winter. The same with Key Bridge, which we opened in 1959. It took us a little while to develop enough marketing muscle to bring in a steady stream of commercial business and small conventions to keep our rooms filled year-round.

Part of our good luck with Twin Bridges and Key Bridge was pure timing. Our lodging business was launched when the American hotel industry was still recovering from World War II. Lodging options for travelers consisted mainly of old city hotels built in the financial heyday of the 1920s or hundreds of tiny mom-and-pop motel operations. When we appeared on the landscape with Twin Bridges in 1957, we were just smart enough to know we had something fresh to offer and just naive enough to go at it with the wide-eyed enthusiasm and energy of a bunch of kids who knew nothing about the business.

One thing our good timing brought us was a little breathing room to figure out just what the devil we were doing. (Remember room service and ice buckets?) When I look back, I have to laugh at how little we knew when we were starting out in lodging. In today's competitive environment, we'd have been eaten alive!

Had I had my way, we would have plowed our energy into building the hotel division faster and sooner than we did. I felt confident that the future promised to be a bright one for new, aggressive hotel companies. The interstate highway system was growing, new office buildings dotted the suburbs, airports were popping up, and general postwar prosperity was kicking up a tidal wave of business and leisure travel.

But Dad and Wall Street had other things in mind. At the time, my father was still dead-set against taking on the scale of debt required to build a lot of big hotels. Wall Street was crazy about conglomerates; analysts constantly wanted to know what new business we were getting into next. So in the early 1970s, we began looking around for additional avenues of growth.

Our next diversification effort was Marriott World Travel, a travel agency launched in 1971. The business played to several of Marriott's strengths and seemed to be a natural outgrowth of our existing businesses. We had a dozen hotels and would soon have three cruise ships and two theme parks. With leisure travel on the upswing, a travel agency seemed perfect for Marriott.

So what was the problem? Probably the most important sticking point was the displeasure of established travel agencies—many of whom could (and did) quickly stop sending clients to anything related to Marriott. In retrospect, we should have seen the potential for conflict. The original team in Marriott World Travel was also a bit too gung-ho for our own good; they committed Marriott to various initiatives and weren't able to follow through. The change they were trying to implement was a little too precocious for the order to absorb. We gave the travel agency business a good effort, but exited in 1979.

The next diversification opportunity came in the shape of cruise ships, a business we got into in 1972. Sun Line provided our first major lesson about the dangers of getting into a completely unfamiliar business. Having diversified successfully and relatively painlessly into hotels fifteen years earlier, we felt confident that we could pull it off. After all, cruise ships were essentially just floating hotels, right? Wrong! Not only were they more complicated than we realized, but we made the error of letting ourselves get into a partnership in which we didn't have the controlling interest. Given our corporate culture based on systems and attention to detail, it drove us crazy not to be calling the shots. It certainly didn't help matters that the Greek islands—the main destination of our ships— were plagued by the Cypriot War our second season! For obvious reasons, people do *not* generally enjoy cruising in a war zone. Before the war started, our ships were full; after the shooting began, cancellations poured in and we had to tie the ships up . . . at the peak of the cruise season. Someone who is more superstitious than I am might say that the war was a bad omen for Sun Line. I will give us credit (or take the blame) for being persistent; we spent fifteen years trying to make a go of it before finally getting out.

At the same moment that we took on the Sun Line challenge, Marriott decided to get into the theme park business. Unlike cruise ships, our foray into theme parks was to be a "ground up" effort. We planned from the start to build them ourselves and not partner with anyone.

Theme parks took advantage of several of our strengths. We grew up in the food service business, were fanatical housekeepers, and were definitely family-oriented. For our two Great America theme parks, we picked high-traffic locations in the San Francisco Bay Area and midway between Milwaukee and Chicago. We slated openings to take advantage of the Bicentennial fervor of 1976.

Our first hard lesson came during construction. Building a park from scratch without any previous experience turned out to be both tricky and expensive. We had become experts in designing and constructing big buildings, but small one-of-a-kind structures that had to conform to another category of building code temporarily threw us for a loop. We had never built a roller coaster, for example; eventually, we constructed six. As soon as they got the hang of it, Marriott's architecture and construction division did a terrific job. The buildings and rides at both parks were wonderful.

Our big mistake about theme parks was not recognizing the amount of money and imagination required on the *entertainment* side of the picture. Adding new rides is extremely capital-intensive; a single ride costs several million dollars. Really good rides—the kind that bring people in by the droves—also require an edgier kind of creative thinking than we had. After several years of doing well, but never feeling entirely comfortable with the business, we sold the properties at a profit and bowed out.

Cruise ships and theme parks were our biggest and most expensive diversification efforts of the 1970s, but not the only ones. One venture that I would gladly forget is our foray into home security systems. It only lasted three years—from 1973 to 1976—and, fortunately, was little more than a blip on Marriott's radar screen. The business simply did not fit us.

The silver lining of our short-lived security enterprise is the lesson it taught: the importance of letting people develop new ideas. The idea itself didn't work for us, but we discovered that our organization was flexible enough to give it a try and resilient enough not to let its failure get in the way of giving other ideas a fair shake. I call that preserving "order amid change . . . and . . . change amid order" at its best.

You've probably noticed that in all of the diversification efforts mentioned so far—with the exception of hotels—I've made the point that we discovered major, ultimately insurmountable, difficulties only *after* getting into the business.

Why have I highlighted that common thread? One of the most valuable lessons we learned in all those ventures—aside from the importance of taking risks and bouncing back—is that when problems arise in a business, you need to know enough about the business to be able to fix them. It's that simple. If you don't understand the business in the first place, you *can't* fix it when it goes wrong. In fact, you might not even be able to figure out what the problem *is*!

In each of the cases I've described, we were guilty to varying degrees of not having done enough homework before plunging in. As a result, we were surprised by problems that might have been avoided or that would have alerted us to steer clear of the business altogether.

What we were experiencing was a growing pain common to businesses trying to extend beyond their original ideas. Our enthusiasm for innovation occasionally got ahead of our organization's ability to absorb and promote healthy experimentation. Among other things, we were trying too many unfamiliar businesses simultaneously.

What was missing at Marriott in the 1960s and

1970s was an organizational structure for analyzing and managing change. Until the late 1970s, my father and I looked at opportunities on a case-by-case basis. If something came up that I thought was worth taking a look at, I would bring it to Dad's attention for a little ad hoc investigation and often heated discussion.

Our informal decision-making methods were in keeping with the company's traditional approach to growth. For the first thirty-odd years of our history, the primary strategic question that came up again and again was by and large limited to picking the right location for a new Hot Shoppe. After we got into airline catering in 1937, the strategy again revolved around location: up-and-coming airports for our flight kitchens. When we got into hotels in the mid-1950s, we were still focused on pretty much the same basic question: Which suburban markets, convention cities, and major transportation hubs did we want to target?

The "location, location, location" planning mind-set was great for building our food and lodging divisions, but fell short of what we needed to analyze new, unfamiliar businesses. Looking back, I see now that the case-by-case approach was partly a reflection of our long-standing orientation (some would say bias) toward operations. It's human nature to favor what you know you can do well and shy away from what you don't like or haven't mastered. In our case, it was our internal inclination to downplay nonoperations activities in favor of the familiar task of making a restaurant or hotel work. We couldn't relate to abstract strategic planning exercises as well as we could to the tangible satisfaction of getting a facility built and filled with customers.

Because of our bias toward operations, we assumed too confidently that there wasn't anything that the company's first-class operators couldn't ultimately figure out how to run. What we learned, of course, is that even the very best operators can't fix a decision that wasn't right in the first place.

By the late 1970s, the moment had arrived to acknowledge that Marriott needed to be more disciplined about analyzing potential business ventures. We established a strategic-planning department. To some degree, we were merely following the trend of the times. But for Marriott, it was also an important step along the road to organizational maturity. We liked change, but had not adapted our order to manage change for our benefit. By harnessing change, the strategic-planning department simultaneously protected—or preserved—it. We took a leap toward achieving the all-important balance between order and change.

Marriott soon learned—maybe in the nick of time—that one of the most valuable roles of a strategic-planning department is to keep a company out of businesses it shouldn't be in. This one benefit alone turned out to be very important for us. As our hotel business grew by leaps and bounds in the late 1970s and 1980s, our cash flow suddenly grew like crazy, too. We were faced with the enviable problem of having to find constructive uses for money. It would have been a snap to throw cash at lots of different businesses. Many companies have gotten themselves into trouble that way—acquiring for the sake of acquiring, launching new enterprises simply because they've got the money to give them a whirl. Before we established our formal strategic-planning department, we were guilty of this. Fortunately, Marriott's group of planners were terrific at sorting out our options and supplying excellent reasons not to get into various businesses.

On the other hand, we didn't suddenly stop diversifying in 1980 just because we got our planning act together. If that had been the case, we would have done little more than churn out full-service hotels while keeping our restaurant and airline catering divisions humming along. We did not sit still; we simply became more thoughtful and studious about analyzing what we got into. Nor did the planners suddenly take control and call the shots. Then as now, I still ultimately make decisions based on intuition and experience, not merely numbers.

Some of what we chose to do in the 1980s was what has been called "sticking to one's knitting." We took a closer look at close-to-home opportunities. On the contract services side of our business (restaurants, food service, etc.)—a full one-half of the company—the decade brought major change, much of it in terms of scale. Among other things, as I mentioned earlier, we lit a fire under our distribution services and turned what had been mostly an internal supply function into a major growth business—one that is projected to reach more than $1.6 billion in annual revenues before the end of 1997.

We also focused our energies on growing our contract food services management operation. My dad had launched the division in the late 1930s when he began catering meals at the U.S. Treasury building in downtown Washington. Over the years, the business had grown in terms of clients, locations, and numbers of customers served, but we had not really focused on it to the degree that we could have. Our new strategic planning mind-set in the 1980s helped us home in on the potential to grow the business. Three key acquisitions (Gladieux, Saga, and Service Systems) during the decade transformed us into one of the biggest players in the industry. By 1989, we had expanded the business more than tenfold in just five years, with accounts in places as close to home as the Lockheed Martin corporate cafeteria in Bethesda, Maryland, and as far-flung as the oil rigs on Alaska's Northern Slope.

We didn't stop there. Next, we built on sixty years of experience in managing clients' cafeterias and dining rooms to expand our portfolio to include a whole range of facilities management services. Marriott Management Services (MMS) provides not only food service but plant operation, laundry, housekeeping, and energy management to hundreds of clients in business, health care, education, and other sectors.

The late 1980s brought other pivotal decisions on the nonlodging side of the company. Specifically, our longest-lived divisions: airline catering and restaurants. After sixty years, we knew a lot about both businesses. And because we knew them so intimately, we came to the difficult, but correct, conclusion in 1989 that both had run their courses for us.

From the standpoint of the balance sheet, the decision to put our restaurants and In-Flite on the block was easy. From the standpoint of the company's corporate culture, it was anything but. Marriott's can-do attitude had been born in the hustle of restaurant life during the Great Depression. A decision to exit our original businesses seemed to cut at the very roots of the company. On another level, however, it was a healthy sign that we recognized the dangers of allowing order to win out over change at the expense of progress. We sold the businesses and moved on.

On the lodging side of Marriott, the 1980s likewise brought incredible changes, led by one development that was perhaps more revolutionary than anything else we've done as an organization. I'm referring to our decision in 1981 to move into other market tiers in the hotel industry. Moderate-priced entry Courtyard by Marriott was the first fruit of that strategic decision.

What's the big deal about a hotel company going into the hotel business? How can that be labeled revolutionary?

For Marriott, Courtyard was a *very* big deal. We had defined ourselves for a quarter of a century as a *full-service* hotel company. We were known for our expertise in building big boxes loaded with lots of bells and whistles. And we *liked* being known for our big boxes. Little boxes were what *other* companies did. Not Marriott, no, never!

Given how entrenched that attitude was within our corporate culture, it's perhaps a little amazing that Courtyard happened at all. The fact that it did is a tribute to two things: one, the dedicated people who worked like crazy to pull it off, and two, the company's maturity as a manager of change. Courtyard was a severe test of our organizational ability to foster innovation—preserve it—at the risk of our cherished core identity.

Courtyard disturbed our status quo the most, because it was a clear case of messing with success. Our other diversification efforts—cruise ships, the travel agency, theme parks, home security—had all been somewhat removed from our bigger and better-known business. In those cases, if we didn't make a stellar showing or if we failed, the damage to our reputation as a hotelier was minimal. Courtyard, on the other hand, had the power to strike right at the heart of the organization. If we blew it, so the arguments ran, we'd lose more than just our investment in Courtyard. We risked twenty-five years of hard work establishing our name in the industry.

The point was a valid one, but not the only one. Balancing the worries about rocking the boat—risking the order—were a couple of very compelling arguments. One was our perennial urge to grow. Tackling other segments of the lodging market would open up vast new territory for increasing our bottom line. The market could only support a certain number of full-service Marriott hotels. The second was the fact that the idea for Courtyard came straight out of our new strategic-planning function. Unlike our earlier diversification efforts, we could bring to bear on Courtyard the kind of discipline and study that would minimize risk and maximize potential. Courtyard was the perfect opportunity to take our new planning function for a spin.

The arguments in favor of change won out. For three years, Courtyard incubated in almost complete secrecy. Those who were involved in its planning went into overdrive putting together focus groups, competitor profiles, mock room layouts, and just about anything and everything that would help to make Courtyard a textbook case of product planning. The hard work paid off. When our small-sized, medium-priced, high-style Courtyard by Marriott was finally unveiled in 1983, it really flew!

Part of Courtyard's successful debut was a reflection of the state of the market. The moderate-priced lodging segment had been in need of a fresh product for some time. But it was also the happy culmination of a thousand battles big and small that had raged inside Marriott for three years between the forces of fear and confidence, the known and unknown, order and change.

Of the myriad issues we wrestled with, naming the product was one of the most interesting and revealing. Choosing "Courtyard" was easy; a survey of customer preference settled the question. The hard part was deciding whether or not to include the word "Marriott" in the name. Skeptics and worriers expressed concern that attaching the Marriott tag to a moderate-priced product would tarnish the full-service brand name. Courtyard devotees argued that the Marriott name was vital to boost the product's profile and enhance its chances of success.

Was this a case of silly semantics or was it a pivotal point in our history? To my mind, it was very much the latter. By adding "by Marriott" to the Courtyard brand, the organization crossed a philosophical line. We demonstrated a willingness to throw the weight of the organization behind an innovation that promised—one way or the other, for good or ill—to redefine the core of Marriott. In doing so, we held our breath. We also affirmed a critical organizational truth: We were quite capable of preserving change amid order.

The confidence and momentum generated by Courtyard's success in the marketplace quickly led us to the next logical step: diversification into almost every segment of the lodging industry. In 1984, we announced plans for Marriott Suites; two years later, we unveiled another entry, economy-priced Fairfield Inn by Marriott. Extended-stay brand Residence Inn was acquired in 1987 and tagged with the Marriott name. More recently, we've moved into other limited-service products and have begun plumbing international markets with different Marriott brands. We doubled our overseas presence and expanded our line by three brands (Renaissance, Ramada, and New World) in a single move when we acquired the

Renaissance Hotel Group for $1 billion in March 1997.

The organizational discipline that made Courtyard by Marriott possible also spilled over into other areas. One of today's major growth platforms for Marriott—Senior Living Services—benefited from the growing pains we went through with Courtyard. The same kind of intense strategic study that forged Courtyard led us to target our country's aging population, evaluate their needs, and create a full range of Marriott products to meet them.

We also put on our new strategic thinking cap to expand Marriott Vacation Club International (MVCI), our time-share division, beginning with the acquisition of American Resorts Group in 1984. Bill Tiefel, president of Marriott Lodging, spearheaded our move into the vacation interval business when he recognized that time-share customers were buying a vacation *experience*, not merely a vacation destination. His realization was critical to our ability to tailor our offerings to give customers what they really wanted, as opposed to what we might have assumed was their wish. For example, the MVCI program gives our time-share owners the flexibility to trade in their time-share vacation for a stay at a Marriott hotel if they prefer.

I've had a ball watching what began as institutional heresy in the early 1980s—Marriott building "little boxes"—turn into one of our major growth engines in the late 1980s and beyond. It's been a terrific reminder that sometimes the only thing stopping you from achieving great things is your own mind-set.

I also think we've learned a couple of other useful lessons in our effort to follow Alfred North Whitehead's formula for institutional equilibrium. One is that you can't really know your strengths and weaknesses until you *test* them. It might look safer and more prudent to avoid pushing the envelope, but, in fact, the opposite is true. Companies that don't risk anything will inevitably find themselves falling behind those that do. You can lead change or it can lead you. The trick is to manage risk productively. Resilience, flexibility, and most of all a willingness to acknowledge mistakes and move on will go a long way toward accomplishing that goal.

The other lesson is that an important element of our maturation as an organization lies in looking for a comfortable *balance* between trying new things and sticking to what we know we do best. Any company that plans to stay in business must also seek this balance. You probably won't ever *find* it, but you can certainly come close.

7

NO TREE GROWS TO THE SKY

No tree grows to the sky.

—FREDERICK DEANE
MARRIOTT DIRECTOR

Sometime toward the end of the 1980s—probably late 1988 or early 1989—I attended a big awards banquet at our Camelback Inn in Scottsdale, Arizona. The purpose of the evening was to honor the real estate developers who had secured the greatest number of sites for new Courtyard, Fairfield Inn, and Residence Inn hotels during the previous twelve months. At the time, we were opening about 100 hotels annually and had plenty of others in various stages of design and construction. Our development pipeline was going full steam, in large part due to the work of the people we were honoring.

The evening was a perfect symbol of the fast-paced, no-holds-barred days of American business in the 1980s. Deal making had been raised to an art during the decade, and deal makers had become the new stars, capturing daily headlines with the scale and scope of their financial wizardry. Billions of dollars were spent and made on friendly mergers and not-so-friendly acquisitions. The stock exchanges here and abroad had a field day.

In the lodging industry, the atmosphere and pace of expansion had likewise become supercharged, fueled in part by new provisions in the federal tax code that encouraged individuals to invest in real estate. About 690,000 rooms were added to the U.S. lodging system during the 1980s, the rate of growth accelerating as the decade wore on. Before long, there seemed to be a hotel on every corner. So many, in fact, and all so filled with guests, that it looked like everyone in America was leaving his or her home and taking up residence in hotels.

As I watched the awards being handed out that night, I found myself thinking about the market explosion that had led all of us to that banquet room. I realized that I was very uncomfortable with what I was seeing and hearing. My intuition told me: "Hey, we'd better look at this. . . ." But everyone else in the room seemed to be so bullish and positive about our business that I set my worry aside and joined in the celebration. After all, all signs at the time were positive. Our hotels were filling up as fast as they could be finished, and capital was plentiful. Why not just keep going?

■

In 1990, the wave of hotel expansion that Marriott had been riding suddenly crashed—thanks to an abrupt tailspin of the U.S. real estate market, the rising tensions in the Middle East, and a recession, together with failing to act on my own deep, but not strongly expressed, concerns about overbuilding. The final straw for Marriott was when the Japanese withdrew as large-scale investors in American real estate after Japan's Nikkei index took a nosedive between January and October 1990.

The price we paid when things went sour was dramatic. We took a major hit on our stock price, had to lay off two entire departments of hard-working people, endured a brief takeover scare, and had the dubious pleasure of reading premature Marriott obituaries in the business media. It was not fun.

Once the smoke cleared, we had another big problem: a backlog of lodging properties that our development team had been dutifully churning out before the real estate market went south. As long as we had been able to sell hotels quickly—never a problem in the 1980s—our develop-build-sell-take-back-a-management-contract growth strategy had worked like a charm. We had sold more than $6 billion in lodging properties in the 1980s. But faced with no buyers for our hotels, we suddenly had a billion dollars' worth of unsold property sitting on our books.

No one was more upset about our fix than I was. After years of listening to my father harp on the evils of debt, I felt like I had single-handedly let him and the company down by allowing us to get so caught up in the gross overbuilding of the business. I could almost hear my late father up above saying, "I told you so."

Our most pressing need in the fall of 1990 was to preserve cash. Our team pulled together and soon found money in many obvious places inside Marriott—places we had ignored when capital was available for the asking. The cash sweep resulted in a reduction of our working capital by more than $100 million in just a few months.

To get the company moving again, we also had to do something about our debt level. But we were determined to avoid dealing with it by doing what many of our competitors who faced similar problems were willing to do: sell good sites and hotels at fire-sale prices. In spite of the fevered pace at which we had snapped up locations in the 1980s, our selections by and large had been fine choices. When the real estate market perked up again, we knew we would be glad we had not let those sites go for a song.

Simply sitting on our hands and waiting for the market to come around again wasn't an option, though. Treading water has never been our style. Besides, the real estate crash had kicked up opportunities that we couldn't ignore. Many competitors' lodging properties were in the hands of banks, the federal Resolution Trust Corporation, and other institutions who knew nothing about hotel management . . . and didn't want to learn. Opportunities abounded for Marriott to pick up management contracts. But to do so, we needed to have our own house in order.

In January 1992, Bill Shaw took over as president of the Marriott Service Group, the nonlodging half of the company. Bill had spent the previous two years in the role of chief financial officer, shepherding us through the worst of our cash-flow problems. To fill the empty slot left by Bill's promotion, we hired Steve Bollenbach. Steve was just finishing up a long-term assignment helping Donald Trump restructure his finances.

This was Steve's second tour of duty with us. He had been Marriott's treasurer for several years in the early 1980s. Steve had the advantage of looking at our debt problem from the unique vantage point of a two-time insider *and* recent outsider. After studying us for a few months, he came up with an idea both natural and radical: Why not split the company in two?

Steve did not invent splits, but his reasoning in our case was novel. The original Marriott Corporation—today called Host Marriott—would be able to retain the company's unsold real estate; the new company—today called Marriott International—would become a pure management company.

The concept of splitting Marriott into two pieces was *natural* in the sense that spin-offs were coming into vogue in the early 1990s. A lot of companies were slimming down in an effort to get back to focusing on their core businesses.

The split was *radical* in that companies customarily spin off their *debt*. Steve's idea was to allow the original sixty-five-year-old Marriott company to keep the real estate—including the debt associated with it—and spin off most of its management services into a new company. The new Marriott International would be virtually debt-free, giving it more flexibility to go after management contracts and get the blood moving again throughout the Marriott enterprise.

Under the split scenario devised by Steve, the two companies would continue to share headquarters, but maintain separate boards of directors, hold separate annual meetings, etc. I would serve as chairman, president, and CEO of Marriott International, while my younger brother, Dick, would become chairman and president of Host Marriott. Steve would serve as Host's CEO. Marriott International would manage Host Marriott's properties under long-term agreements.

From a practical viewpoint, the idea made good sense. In one bold move, Marriott could take care of both of its most important immediate goals. Our real estate investments would be managed by one company, the sole business of which was real estate, while our hotel and contract services management skills could be marketed aggressively by the other company.

Important as the plan's practical aspects were, there was another dimension to the split that reached more deeply into the heart of our problems. Splitting the company into two separate entities would fix something fundamental that had gone askew during the heady days just before the 1990 crash. In the aggressive atmosphere of the 1980s, we had let ourselves get pulled too far away from who we really were. Steve's plan would get us back to our core identity: Marriott was (and is) *not* about debt, real estate ownership, and deals; we're about *management and service.*

Marriott needs to make *some* deals, of course. Our recent acquisition of the Renaissance Hotel Group is a good example. But we're definitely at our best and most comfortable when we're up to our ears in operations and feel like we're really *building* something, not just moving assets around on a balance sheet. Where Marriott had gone off-track in the 1980s was in letting development drive the organization rather than support it. In the change-order dynamic, Marriott had lost the critical balance between the two.

Looking back now at the split, there's a delicious irony in having Steve, one of the best deal-makers of our time, craft a state-of-the-art deal designed to move us away from our lopsided tilt toward deal-making and back toward our real identity. But perhaps it's appropriate, too. Sometimes it takes an old friend who knows you well and has seen you in good moments and bad to remind you of who you really are.

When Chariot—the code name for the split—was announced in October 1992, I was prepared for the novelty of the plan to raise some eyebrows. I was not ready for an intensely negative reaction in certain quarters. The main charge we faced was that of acting in bad faith toward our bondholders.

The criticism was pretty upsetting, largely because I didn't think it was well founded. While Marriott has never been a pushover, we're not a bully either; we value our reputation as a "white hat" kind of company. Steve and our legal department (headed by Sterling Colton, our general counsel and son of my father's original partner, Hugh Colton) had been fastidious about crafting the plan for the split to adhere to the law. Even so, we had to face inevitable lawsuits, eventually settling them to all parties' satisfaction.

In the midst of the fireworks I remained convinced that the decision to split was the right one. Our shareholders agreed, voting at our annual meeting in July 1993 to accept the plan by an 85 percent margin.

Three months later, the two companies became official. Just two years after that, Host Marriott split into Host Marriott and Host Marriott Services. The reasoning again was to enhance the ability of the two entities to distinguish missions and goals. Host Marriott remains a real estate company; Host Marriott Services handles food and concession services at airports, shopping centers, toll roads, and sports facilities. Interestingly enough, the second split barely raised an eyebrow. The novelty—and controversy—of splitting had worn off. Since then, all three Marriott companies have been thriving, each doing what it does best.

Now that the dust has long since settled, it's much easier to look back at that topsy-turvy period and appreciate some of its less dramatic aspects. Among other things, we had learned a basic truth, one that Rick Deane, a banker and Marriott director, was fond of pointing out at board meetings. "No tree grows to the sky," he used to say, a warning that even the healthiest growth can't go on forever. Nor can it continue at the fast pace that marks a sapling's first few years. But by splitting the company into pieces—pruning and transplanting, if you will—we had given ourselves new room to grow.

There's one other thing that stands out in my mind from that period. In the midst of the trauma of splitting and rediscovering ourselves, we instituted a small change at headquarters that, on the surface, doesn't look like much—certainly not compared to the headline-making split—but it best captures what we learned from our all-out growth days.

In 1993, we changed the name of Marriott's main decision-making group from the finance committee to the corporate growth committee.

Why do I consider this semantic shift so important?

Like the decision to add "by Marriott" to Courtyard's name, the decision to drop the word "finance" represented a philosophical turning point for us. The term "finance" immediately calls to mind financial engineering and deal-making. The fact that our decision-making group was called by that name in the 1980s says a lot about our priorities and self-image at the time. In contrast, the term "growth" encompasses more than just money. Finance is not emphasized at the expense of other aspects of the business; it's just one of many factors. With that simple wording change, we got back to highlighting what really makes Marriott tick—growth in *all* its permutations, not merely as measured by lines of credit or old-fashioned ticker tape.

8

NEVER BELIEVE YOUR OWN HYPE—OR WHAT THE PRESS SAYS ABOUT YOU

> Nothing is easier than self-deceit. For what each man wishes, that he also believes to be true.
>
> —DEMOSTHENES

Overconfidence is such a destructive force for individuals and institutions that I think it's worth devoting a short chapter to the topic. Companies big and small, new and old, can all fall victim to it; the more successful, the more likely one is to suffer from it. As Marriott learned, there's a price to be paid for thinking too well of yourself.

A pointed reminder of our overconfidence in the 1980s came up recently in a conversation I was having with a colleague at another major hotel company. This fellow told me about a conference he had attended in 1989 at which the hot topic was concern about potential overbuilding in the lodging industry. At one point in the session, a senior Marriott executive announced to a crowd of recession-spooked hotel industry leaders that Marriott was "so powerful, we can build through any cycle."

The statement makes me wince today. I didn't attend the conference my colleague was referring to, but I'm not surprised that someone from Marriott at that point in time could have delivered such a cavalier pronouncement. We'd been riding high for more than a decade and had gotten quite accustomed to setting our own agenda and controlling our fate. Everything had been going so well for us, it appeared that we could do no wrong.

The word "appeared" is key. Tempting as it is, perception should never be confused with reality. Our success was not an illusion, but the attitude that the company might be immune to industry cycles certainly was. It's not only arrogant but foolhardy for any company to think that it will be the exception to the rule of market forces. We discovered that fact the hard way in 1990.

Overconfidence can cause you to misread signals about which you might normally worry. On one hand, the speed of the real estate market crash of 1990 and the outbreak of the Persian Gulf War early in 1991 took lots of people by surprise, not just Marriott. On the other hand, there were suggestions of potential trouble that we might have picked up on . . . and reacted to. The hotel industry media had been filled for months with worried discussions about overbuilding. The conference I just mentioned revolved around the same fears. All the while, our annual reports continued to express our confidence that we were so big and self-sufficient that an industry shakeout was not likely to affect us.

Danger signals weren't just flashing for smaller companies, though. They were flashing for the big ones, too. The unveiling of our first Fairfield Inn syndication in November 1989 was greeted unenthusiastically by a Wall Street that had always eagerly gobbled up earlier Marriott offerings. We sold the syndication, but not as quickly as previous deals.

Looking back almost ten years later with all the advantage of hindsight, I see now that we probably could have turned off the hotel development pipeline about a year earlier than we did and blunted some (but not all) of the troubles of 1990. But in the hard-charging atmosphere that had developed at Marriott—and the industry as a whole—in the 1980s, we truly believed that we were pursuing a virtually puncture-proof strategy for growth.

Most evidence pointed to that upbeat conclusion. Every week, we were holding opening parties for new hotels—hotels that filled up as soon as the doors opened. Our stock soared; our shareholders were thrilled. The latter years of the decade melded together into one big, 'round-the-clock celebration at Marriott. If a hardy soul *had* insisted on raining on our parade, we probably would have smothered both the message and the messenger in cake and champagne. Of course, *I* was the one leading the parade, and I was having almost as much fun as everyone else. The buck stopped with me.

When the party broke up in 1990, one comfort lay in knowing that business of any kind is always a risk. Whether you're in business for yourself or in partnership with others, no one can be 100 percent certain that things will turn out as planned. There are simply too many variables and uncontrollable forces at work. All you can do is calculate the risk as best you can, decide whether you're up to it, accept that no strategy is foolproof, and recover from mistakes as gracefully as possible.

In the aftermath of the 1990 crash, we've taken off the party hats, put away the noisemakers, and now listen more closely than ever to colleagues, industry reports, and a host of other indicators that together give us a realistic picture of what's going on. We also have, I hope, learned to keep our corporate ego in check.

One thing that was particularly painful to bear when we hit hard times was the negative press. The media's coverage of the company's problems in 1990 to 1991 and the controversial split into two companies in 1992 to 1993 made for pretty tough reading. The media had fed Marriott's ego in the late 1980s with glowing coverage of the company's growth; it was not surprising that the press was equally quick to be critical when the company stumbled. The episode was a good reminder that it's dangerous to read your own press clippings and take them seriously.

Ultimately, what saved us from a terminal case of arrogance was something I've talked about at many points in this book: our corporate culture. The company owes a debt of gratitude to the confidence—not *over*confidence—of loyal Marriott associates who came together and worked hard to bring the company back from the brink to its better instincts.

In fact, the company's worst days brought out the best in the organization, even while putting our core values to the test. A long tradition of teamwork and a healthy track record of taking care of each other helped to keep us from falling apart, as could easily have been the case. Instead of jumping ship, thousands of people pulled together across the country and around the world to help us right ourselves.

In addition to helping us find ways to cut our working capital by $100 million, associates toughed out a salary freeze in 1991. Senior executives—approximately 1,100—had their pay frozen for the entire year. Some also sacrificed their annual bonuses. Middle managers—about 5,000 people—had their salaries frozen for six months. All other managers and our administrative/clerical associates endured a three-month freeze. Our hourly payroll associates were not affected.

Like their reaction to the layoff of the development and architectural and construction divisions, the attitude of associates toward our financial predicament was far more understanding than I think many companies would have enjoyed in the same situation. At headquarters and in the field, people signaled their belief that the decision to freeze salaries would not have been made if it had not been necessary. They also responded positively to the approach we used. The "weighting" of the freeze timetable put the biggest burden on those most able to bear it. Finally, there was general compassion for our problems and a recognition that we weren't the only company having troubles. Corporate America as a whole was having to suck it up a bit after a decade of wild growth.

Marriott is still staffed today by many associates

who lived through those challenging days with us. Their experience and memories of the slim times are, for the moment, our most effective check against "arrogance creep." But we can't depend on those associates being around forever to make sure that we don't let future successes go to our heads. Other kinds of vigilance are needed as well.

Among other things, we must continue to build and maintain a corporate culture that values and celebrates success, but remains capable of critical self-analysis. We've already touched upon some of the elements that I personally think are important to our corporate culture: good listening skills, attention to detail, putting employees first, maintaining equilibrium between the forces of change and the status quo. Others like teamwork, managing big egos and ambition, and valuing your partners in success will be explored in upcoming chapters. All of these factors are critical to keeping the system as a whole in healthy balance.

Perhaps the most important check against overconfidence in an institution is the quality that protects human beings from the same fate: a sense of humor. Being able to laugh at yourself once in a while is a good thing.

When Chariot was picked as the code name for our plans to split the company in 1993, we didn't give much thought to the choice. Any major project that a business undertakes usually gets tagged with a convenient name until a permanent one, if needed, is dreamed up. The code names range from silly to serious. The fact that Chariot rhymed with Marriott was a nice touch, but essentially meaningless. The image of Roman warriors lent a note of nobility, but likewise didn't say a whole lot.

When we found ourselves dragged into battle with our bondholders over the proposed split, the name's connotations of war suddenly took on an unintended, somewhat humorous significance. Best of all, a pundit in the company redubbed the project "Chariot of Fire," a tongue-in-cheek reference to the popular 1981 movie. Years later, the pun still makes me roll my eyes; it *also* never fails to give me a good chuckle.

9

VALUE THE ORGANIZATION MORE THAN INDIVIDUAL PLAYERS

> All for one, one for all, that is our motto.
>
> —ALEXANDRE DUMAS THE ELDER
> *THE THREE MUSKETEERS*

Much of what you've read so far in this book might lead you to assume that everyone at Marriott always works cheerfully and unfailingly for the good of the whole. In general, that's remarkably true. Teamwork is a hallmark of our corporate culture. It's one of the company's many strengths that I'm most proud of.

At the same time, the fact that we're able to get nearly 225,000 associates to march in the same general direction on any given day does not mean that we have miraculously escaped dealing with maverick human nature. We haven't. Nor does it signify that the company is staffed by yes-men, robots, or mindless conformists. We're not.

The strength of Marriott's teamwork ethic simply means that we've successfully created an environment in which the rewards for working together outweigh those of working for one's own interest.

How did we accomplish this? Before I get to that, let me tell you about a brief period in the company's history when teamwork was not the order of the day. Although the situation didn't last long, the episode is worth highlighting because for us, it was the exception that proves the rule.

The trouble stemmed from a rivalry between two particularly ambitious Marriott executives. The situation arose when the company underwent one of its periodic restructurings designed to give a few people the opportunity to try on new organizational "hats." Both men began eyeing the same hat.

Given the personalities of the two, I was prepared for a certain amount of friction, but the competition quickly took on the characteristics of a blood match, marked by heavy muscling and back-channel agendas.

It would have been bad enough if the negative impact of the competition had been limited only to those two individuals. But people who worked with or close to them got caught in the fallout of their machinations. Judgment, morale, and productivity all suffered. No one—including the two executives—came out a winner. Neither got the hat he was hoping for. Both eventually left the company and found positions in other organizations.

The episode underscored a couple of fundamental truths. One, in a people-oriented business like Marriott's, it's critical to get the "people" part right. Both of the executives were bright, capable, hands-on managers, but instead of taking care of each other and those who worked for and with them—a key tenet of our teamwork-based culture—they let personal priorities get the upper hand. In the process, they destroyed a great deal of goodwill, wasted energy, and upset a lot of people.

The second truth illuminated by the contest of egos is that our corporate culture is at heart an egalitarian one. As an organization, we have a low tolerance for big shots. An emphasis on title and privilege goes against our grain. Those who put themselves the most forward have been, in general, the least likely to get ahead.

This brings to mind the story of how we got the teamwork ethic in the first place. When we were just starting out in the late 1920s, few, if anyone, in the company had special credentials. Everyone scrambled and worked hard; everyone also had a fair shot at moving up the ladder. Dedication and street smarts were more apt to win someone a promotion than academic degrees, the "right" connections, or a knack for playing institutional politics. By the time American business became credential-conscious after World War II, Marriott's "everybody-roll-up-your-sleeves-and-pitch-in" mind-set was already a cornerstone of the company's culture.

The result was a workplace that wasn't—and still isn't—a terribly comfortable environment for outsized egos or title-seekers. Not that we don't have plenty of well-trained professionals in our ranks today. Nor does it mean that we don't have our share of superstar talent. We definitely do, including some exceptionally savvy people who have since gone on to other exciting challenges. While they were at Marriott, however, they were not handled with kid gloves.

Creating a teamwork-oriented culture is one thing, maintaining it is another. One thing that I think contributes to keeping the teamwork concept strong at Marriott is the fact that we're not willing to dangle outrageous incentive packages in front of talented people to keep them on board as long as possible. We depend too much upon people working *together* toward a common goal to risk fracturing the team by setting up a reward structure that distinguishes a few disproportionately. *Everyone* who works for the company is making a contribution to our success. There would be no quicker way to jeopardize, if not destroy, the special "we're-in-this-together" ambience of our workplace than by recognizing a few folks beyond their market value.

Does that mean companies like ours that have an egalitarian outlook have to forfeit the benefit of regular injections of superstar talent? Not at all. But it does require finding ways to *balance* (a word I've used again and again) the needs of the institution against the needs of "home-run hitters."

One of the most important, positive decisions a company can make is to welcome smart, ambitious people. Every business needs them to drive it into the future. Ambitious people have egos; they must have confidence in their abilities. What's important is whether or not they know how to manage their egos. If they don't, the system must be strong enough to manage it for them. That means keeping a check on their ability to affect others adversely.

It's also important to promote an open environment in which *everyone* can be creative. Those executives who truly crave off-the-charts financial rewards will eventually leave anyway, but you'll still have plenty of others for whom the challenge of the job—the opportunity to be imaginative and to contribute—will be more enticing than money.

Avoid allowing competitive rivalries to creep into the organization. It's important not to reward maverick behavior with promotions, attention, or money if the behavior costs the institution something fundamental. (On the other hand, do reward creativity and innovative thinking!) Encourage teamwork. It keeps the system in balance, reduces competition, and squelches agendas that aren't in the larger interest.

Finally, value the organization more than individual players. If your company's structure and corporate culture are both strong, the institution should be able to withstand the comings and goings of ambitious people. You never want the organization to be held hostage by the creativity or drive of a single individual or small cadre of hotshots. In that sense, a healthy company is a bit like a good marriage. No one has the upper hand, special talents and contributions are respected and appreciated, and all concerned know that the whole is worth far more than the sum of its parts.

Over the years, I've watched the separate parts of Marriott evolve into a strong corporate marriage. On the lodging side, for example, when we first started diversifying in the mid-1980s, each segment ran its own show independent of the others. The brands competed with one another for customers and didn't share resources or automatically refer guests to one another. That changed in the early 1990s when Bill Tiefel, head of our lodging group, orchestrated a merger of all of our lodging businesses into a single "brand-management" structure. Each Marriott lodging line now has its own brand manager who makes sure that the integrity and uniqueness of the brand remains intact.

The most important fallout of the restructuring is the way the brands have embraced working *together*. During the first year under the new structure, the brands referred more than $170 million in business to one another. Now *that's* teamwork!

10

SUCCESS IS A TEAM SPORT

No man is an island, entire of itself;
every man is a piece of the continent . . .

—JOHN DONNE

As of this printing, Marriott International employs 225,000 associates—and counting. We're the thirteenth largest employer in the United States. We're also the biggest hotel management company in the world. The company dishes up millions of breakfasts, lunches, and dinners a year through our hotel restaurants and 3,500 food service units. Our distribution arm delivers 1.7 million cases of food-related products around the country each week. And more than 15,000 senior citizens reside in our retirement communities. As a whole, we purchase more groceries, make more beds, and serve more meals than any other enterprise, with the possible exception of the military.

A company Marriott's size seems tailor-made to call to mind the classic joke: "Where does a 500-pound gorilla sit?" Answer: "Anywhere it wants."

The real joke is on any company that believes sheer size should secure it special privileges. Size guarantees nothing—nothing except plenty of challenges to keep moving ahead.

As I've watched Marriott grow and change over the years, I've concluded that one of the most serious battles for large companies is the fight against "thinking big." I don't mean in the sense of dreaming big dreams or chasing big ideas. I mean the problem of letting an organization's large size become an excuse for complacency, self-satisfaction, arrogance, and passing the buck.

In an organization that has thousands of people and hundreds of locations, it doesn't take much for bureaucracy to creep in and strangle initiative. Ideas can get lost in a maze of official channels. Employees can lose faith in their ability to make a difference, so they stop trying. Or figure someone else will pick up the slack if they fail to pull their weight.

Those challenges are often compounded by the fact

that big organizations can easily fall prey to isolation. Large companies tend to become their own mini-nations, their "citizens" bound together by special vocabularies, "governments," and, of course, unique cultures. At Marriott, for example, we've got a guide to company acronyms that runs nine pages! Internal meetings often sound like they're being conducted in a foreign language thanks to the shorthand Marriott-speak we've developed and become accustomed to.

When faced with the problems of "thinking big," one of the most effective counterattacks, I believe, is to remind yourself constantly, vigilantly, and diligently that your success didn't happen in a vacuum. We came very close to forgetting that truth during the late 1980s.

Any successful business needs—and will always need—a lot of people, both inside and outside, to make it a winner. We have literally millions of partners in success. First, we have our team of associates, our most valued players. Then we have our property owners, our stockholders, our bondholders, Wall Street, our peers and competitors, our franchisees, and, of course, our customers. *Everyone* plays a role in making Marriott what it is.

I've said again and again that our associates are number one. It won't hurt to say it one more time. Without the hard work and dedication of our team, Marriott wouldn't exist. Period. That's why taking care of our employees is a top priority for the organization. It's also the reason why the kind of destructive personal rivalry that I talked about in the last chapter is heartily discouraged and ultimately doomed to fail. And it's why I'm such a fanatic about having upbeat, involved, hands-on managers in every corner of the company. Every single person who works for Marriott should be excited to be a member of our organization.

How do you accomplish that goal when you've got hundreds of thousands of associates scattered around the globe? I talked in Chapter 3 about many of the employee-oriented programs, initiatives, and attitudes that Marriott has undertaken over the years: training, work-life programs, safety nets, profit sharing, and a bias toward promotion from within. These visible signs all contribute—I hope—to giving our associates the message that Marriott recognizes that they're central to the company's success.

Recognition also takes the form of celebrating our associates' contributions. At the companywide level, we've instituted an Associate Appreciation Day to remind everyone in Marriott on the same date, at the same time, that we're all in this adventure together. Parties, contests, special awards, and a lot of heartfelt thanking fills the day. The response has been so positive that we've expanded the program to a week's worth of activities.

One special event that takes place in conjunction with Associate Appreciation Day is the J. Willard Marriott Award of Excellence, named after my father and designed to honor our associates who go the extra mile on a regular basis. We've had associates from every walk of Marriott life win this honor: front desk clerks, van drivers, bakers, housekeepers, banquet assistants, and so on. This award is a true pleasure to bestow, because it recognizes people who epitomize the best aspects of Marriott's culture. It's a particularly important event, because the award recognizes our workers in operations, *not* our executives.

Another high-profile honor, given out on the lodging side of the company, is the Tiefel Award, named after our lodging group president, Bill Tiefel. Established in 1989, the award recognizes extraordinary service rendered by associates to guests and, on occasion, to one another. Tiefel Awards are given out throughout the year and are often triggered by a letter or other communication from a guest who praises an associate for service above and beyond the call of duty. Those selected receive a plaque and letter of thanks from Bill Tiefel. They are also honored in special ceremonies at their home properties.

Yet another corporate honor is the Alice S. Marriott Award for Community Service, founded in 1992 and named after my mother. Unlike the Award of Excellence and the Tiefel Award, this program recognizes not individuals but operating units of Marriott that have made outstanding contributions to their communities. The idea is to encourage Marriott associates to band together to help the company be a good corporate citizen in the locales in which we operate.

As important as companywide recognition programs are, it's even more critical to make associate appreciation a daily, ongoing, bone-deep philosophy. Celebrating the successes of associates should be every manager's daily goal. After all, their success is Marriott's success.

Every Marriott property has its own way of thanking and recognizing associates, but one of my favorites is the Hospitality Gold Star program at one of our vacation resorts. Each week, three guests are selected at random and asked to identify the Marriott associate who has been most helpful during their stay. Each guest receives a beach towel as a gift for helping out. The associates who are identified by the guests receive a monetary award, plus gold stars to wear on their uniforms. Simple enough, right? But there's a twist. The three winning associates are then asked to identify three associates in the heart of the house who have been most helpful to *them* during the week. That trio of associates likewise receives monetary awards and gold stars.

Why the second round of awards? The GM at the property knows that the folks on the front lines could not do their jobs and win guest plaudits and gold stars without the support of the people working behind the scenes. The second three awards make sure that heart of the house contributions don't go unrecognized or unrewarded simply because they're invisible to most guests.

In addition to our associates, Marriott's financial stakeholders are also partners in our success. Shareholders, banks, and other investors may not be as visible in the daily life of the company as our associates and our customers, but they are extremely important to us. Not only do they contribute the financing that makes it possible for the company to grow, but they supply faith in our ability and drive to make things happen. It never hurts to remember that no one is forcing people to invest in us—they ante up because we've promised to deliver.

When Marriott went public in 1953, our first offering sold out in less than two hours. If my father needed any assurance that his company was on the right track, that fast-and-furious display of confidence supplied it. More than forty years later, we still have some of those original stockholders, plus many thousands of newer ones, including associates who belong to the company's profit sharing program. Our financial stakeholders provide us with plenty of incentive for doing the best we can to pay them back with continued growth and consistently strong earnings. And as any public company knows, they'll be the first to let us know if we're disappointing them.

Were you surprised to see peers and competitors on the list of partners in success? Competitors are often your best motivators and, consequently, a key factor in your success.

When Marriott decided to go after the limited-service segments of the lodging market in the early 1980s, the specter of competition was a critical factor in our planning. We weren't too worried about the complacent companies that weren't likely to rally in response to Courtyard by Marriott, we were worried about what our nimble and aggressive competitors would do the moment we were out of the gate. Part of the excitement of Courtyard's development was the secrecy we maintained until we unveiled the product. The reward was knowing that many of the first few months' guests staying in our initial Courtyard hotels were our competitors, checking us out!

Even while competitors are keeping you on your toes in the marketplace, keep in mind that your rivals are also your peers. The old saying rings true: "What goes around comes around." If you hold yourself above your competition, you risk isolating yourself and losing out on sources of help when you need it most.

We work constantly with other hospitality companies to deal with local, state, and national issues that affect our industries. Team effort takes place under the umbrella of our various trade associations. But many meaningful collaborations take place on a more ad hoc basis. Sometimes it's as simple as one hotel helping out free of charge when the other's laundry service breaks down. Other joint ventures are more strategic. Just to give you an example, Marriott and two other lodging companies have jointly opened and heavily subsidized a child-care center in Atlanta to be used by the city's lodging industry as a whole. By sharing costs and promoting industrywide involvement in employee work-life programs, everyone benefits—the companies, the employees, and the kids.

Our franchisees constitute yet another important set of Marriott partners. After a long history of being somewhat shy toward the lodging franchise community, we're thrilled to find so many opportunities today to ally with companies and individuals who want to be part of the Marriott family. Our partnerships with our franchisees really *are* partnerships; both sides make significant contributions to create and sustain the relationship. Among other things, our franchisees must share our bias for action, long-term vision, and values. They must be willing to live up to the same high standard of customer satisfaction that we expect of ourselves. To help them achieve that goal, we provide franchise properties with the same resources and support that we know from our own experience are critical to succeed, flourish, and grow.

Last but not least among our partners in success are the millions of customers who use our services. We certainly wouldn't exist without the people who choose to stay in our hotels, retire to our senior living centers, dine in our cafeterias, or vacation at our resorts. They've got plenty of alternatives, and we know it!

Like our competitors, our customers keep us hopping. Part of what gets us out of bed in the morning is the search for new ways to keep them happy, earn their loyalty, and win *more* customers. I'm the first to admit that providing food and shelter doesn't qualify as rocket science, but there have been plenty of things we've pioneered or tweaked over the years in the name of improving customer service.

Some of our more recent innovations have focused on trying to help guests get in and out of our hotels faster and on to the business or pleasure that brought them to us in the first place. One is the in-room video checkout service that we initiated in the early 1980s. By 1986, the service was in use in fifty of our hotels and spread from there. But before in-room video, we instituted Express Checkout that keeps our nighttime associates prowling the halls as they slip a bill under every departing guest's door by 4:00 A.M. Today, customers shouldn't have to go near the front desk on their way out the door.

To improve the experience at the other end of the guest's stay, we unveiled our First Ten program in 1991. The idea was to eliminate the need for guests to stand in line at the front desk. First Ten ended the practice of handing off guests during the crucial first ten minutes after their arrival. Remember the importance of the human touch? When guests first come in the door of a hotel, they're usually exhausted from travel and anxious to get to their rooms and recoup. How their needs are handled during the first few minutes after stepping out of the cab or parking the car forms a lasting impression of our ability to help them pull it all together again. First Ten puts an arriving guest into the hands of just one person, who greets the guest at the door, key in hand, and ushers the newcomer to a room. It's a small touch, but an important one.

One of the most sweeping customer-service innovations we've introduced is our Marriott Rewards frequent traveler program. If you stay at Marriott hotels (and I hope you do), you might already be familiar with one or more of the stand-alone frequent-stay pro-

Photography Credit: Courneye Tourcotte

J. W. Marriott, Jr., with his father and company founder, J. Willard.

All family photographs, unless otherwise noted, courtesy of the Marriott family.

ABOVE LEFT:
Richard E. Marriott (left) and J. W. Marriott, Jr., with their mother, Alice S. Marriott.

ABOVE RIGHT: Bill, Christmas 1933.

BOTTOM:
J. Willard Marriott and son Bill; New Hampshire, 1937.

LEFT:
Bill on his way to becoming an Eagle Scout.

BELOW LEFT:
Bill (left) with his brother, Dick.

BELOW RIGHT:
Left to right: J. Willard Marriott, Alice S. Marriott, Dick (rear), and Bill.

Bill in the U.S. Navy in 1955 as a service supply officer on the air-craft carrier USS *Randolph*.

The company's second hotel, the Key Bridge Marriott, opened in 1959. Alice Marriott, Donna Marriott, and Bill watch as J. Willard Marriott and actress Dina Merrill help granddaughter Debbie cut the ribbon.

Marriott celebrates grand opening of its 100th hotel, the Maui Marriott Resort.

Marriott is listed for the first time on the New York Stock Exchange in 1968.

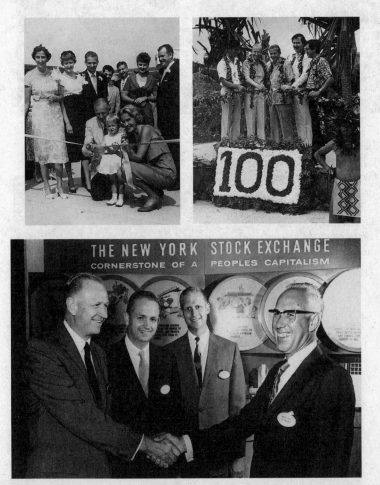

ABOVE:
J. W. Marriott, Jr., supports the Easter Seals Society.

RIGHT:
J. W. Marriott, Jr., makes one of many visits to the company's hotels to tour and check on operations.

LEFT:
Bill and wife, Donna.

BELOW LEFT:
Bill, with Mike Reagan, attempts to break world speed record in "Assault on the Mississippi."

BELOW RIGHT:
Bill takes time out to play a round of golf.

Bill and family:
SEATED (LEFT TO RIGHT):
daughter Debbie and son David
STANDING (LEFT TO RIGHT):
son John, wife Donna, and son Stephen.

The 1,500-room San Francisco Marriott, which opened in 1989, features 85,000 square feet of meeting space and seven restaurants and lounges.

All business-related photographs courtesy of Marriott International, Inc.

ABOVE LEFT:
The lobby of the JW Marriott Hotel Dubai, an elegant 239-room property that opened in 1993 in the United Arab Emirates.

ABOVE RIGHT:
The lobby of the Marriott CasaMagna resort in Cancun, Mexico.

BOTTOM:
Marriott entered the Pacific Rim in 1989 with the opening of the 577-room JW Marriott Hotel in Hong Kong.

TOP:

The elegant 252-room Costa Rica Marriott Hotel opened in San Jose in 1996.

BOTTOM:

The historic Marriott Plaza Hotel in Buenos Aires, Argentina, is located in the heart of the city's premier shopping district.

ABOVE:
Residence Inn is the top U.S. extended-stay lodging brand, appealing to travelers who need a room for five or more consecutive nights.

LEFT:
The beautiful 413-room Aruba Marriott Resort is part of the company's worldwide expansion program aimed at attracting international travelers, who are becoming increasingly brand conscious.

PICTURED AT LEFT:
Courtyard, the company's moderate-priced lodging product, first debuted in 1983 and is the brand preferred by value-conscious individuals and business travelers.

Fairfield Inn is the leader in the economy hotel segment, providing superior value to travelers on a budget.

TOP: Marriott's Forum at Deer Creek in Deerfield Beach, Florida, provides personalized care and assistance to seniors from a well-trained and supportive staff.

ABOVE LEFT: Marriott's Cypress Harbor, one of the company's time-sharing resorts in Orlando, Florida.

ABOVE RIGHT: Marriott's golf division manages 18 U.S. golf facilities for Marriott resorts.

TOP: Marriott Management Services provides food service and facilities management to hospitals throughout the country.

ABOVE: Marriott Distribution Services provides a wide range of food products and supplies to external clients such as Disneyland.

LEFT: Marriott is a leader in providing facilities management services to healthcare facilities in the United States.

The elegant 306-room Ritz-Carlton, Marina Del Rey offers panoramic views of the Pacific Ocean.

grams associated with our hotel brands. Our first program—Marriott Honored Guest Awards—was started in 1983 and quickly became the industry leader. Guests at our hotels, resorts, and suites earn points for every visit. These points can then be applied to future room nights, cruises, and other options. We complement Honored Guest Awards with one of the industry's first frequent-flyer programs, Marriott Miles, as well as a special Club Marquis membership for our most frequent guests. When Marriott diversified into other lodging segments in the 1980s, we added Courtyard Club (Courtyard by Marriott) and INNsiders Club (Fairfield Inn).

By themselves, each of our frequent-stay programs gave our guests nice incentives to come back to us again and again. But the new Marriott Rewards initiative (rolled out in 1997) combines our separate programs into a *single* program. Why? Because customers asked for it! By listening to our guests, we learned that many of our customers choose one brand of Marriott hotel for business travel and another when they're on vacation or looking for a luxurious weekend getaway. The Marriott Rewards program allows guests to earn points at almost any property in our system and apply those points to stays at almost any other—regardless of brand.

These innovations—Express Checkout, First Ten,

Marriott Rewards—were all galvanized by our drive to bring guests back to Marriott. But simply wanting people to come back is no guarantee that good customer service ideas will miraculously appear. The success of our service innovations grows out of two of our most fundamental corporate values: attention to detail and good listening skills. Those cornerstones of our corporate culture—*plus* millions of paying guests—provide ample inspiration for innovation.

The bottom line on partners in success? Never take them for granted. Remember: You exist because of them.

11

LISTEN TO YOUR HEART—AND DON'T LOOK BACK

Not to decide is to decide.

—HARVEY COX

First ponder, then dare.

—HELMUTH VON MOLTKE

In 1965, Marriott opened its fifth hotel, a 500-room convention facility two blocks east of historic Peachtree Street in downtown Atlanta, Georgia. The huge project was designed to put Marriott on the map as a hotel company, and we poured all of our energies into creating a showcase property. Just as we were putting on the finishing touches, we learned that another hotel under construction not far away was up for sale. At the invitation of the architect and developer John Portman, a team of Marriott hotel people toured the site.

Our guys shook their heads over the work flow of the heart of the house. They craned their necks and squinted to find the tip-top of an open-air, multistory space in the central lobby that wasted thousands of cubic feet. They exchanged glances over the confusing location of restaurants and ballrooms. Other aspects of the unusual design came in for silent censure as well.

"It's a disaster! The building will *never* work! We'd have to be crazy to buy it!" was the group's considered opinion. Besides, who would want to have *two* hotels of the same brand in one city? Insane!

We politely declined to make an offer.

Out of our "wisdom" was born the Hyatt Regency of today.

As soon as the Atlanta Hyatt Regency threw open its doors, a steady stream of people passed through the hotel simply to stand in the "Awesome!" spot in the lobby—the best vantage point for appreciating the dizzying heights of the light-filled atrium. In no time, almost every major city decided it needed to have a similar showplace hotel. Hyatt Regencies soon sprouted up in key markets around the country. All because Marriott (among others) couldn't see past the building's unusual mechanics to the architect's grander vision.

To rub salt in the wound, our certainty then that having *two* Marriott hotels in the same city was a crazy idea is now laughable. Today, we have nearly fifty Marriott hotels in the Atlanta area alone!

When I can stop grimacing long enough, I like to use the Atlanta Hyatt Regency story as an example of just one of the thousands of forks in the road that Marriott has faced over the years. Most forks have been small decisions that simply keep the daily grind grinding along. But once in a while, we've been presented with a choice that turns out to have dramatic consequences. As we learned in Atlanta more than thirty years ago, you can't always tell which decisions are which until long after the choice has been made. All you can do is make the best decision possible at that moment, cross your fingers, and keep moving.

Making decisions, of course, is a big part of running a business. Not a day goes by in the life of a company that you don't commit yourself to a particular path, turning down one or more opportunities in favor of another. I've found that following a few simple rules keeps me from getting bogged down by the dozens of puzzles, queries, and opportunities that land on my desk every day.

The first and most important rule is: Be willing to *make* a decision. Not everybody finds this easy. My father *hated* making decisions, for fear that some better option was just around the corner. He analyzed things to death, believing that one more fact or figure could make all the difference between the right decision and a wrong one. Through the years, I spent hours responding to a steady onslaught of detailed comments and concerns from him about every aspect of our business.

Dad's constant barrage of questions drove me a little crazy. If I had stopped to answer his every inquiry, I would never have gotten anything else accomplished. On the other hand, some of the points he raised did help me sharpen my own arguments for the decisions I was making on behalf of the company.

Watching and working with my father for years, I determined not to suffer from the same kind of indecisiveness that plagued him. In fact, I'm sometimes accused—probably with some justification—of being very impatient about making decisions. It's probably a natural reaction to my father, a case of the pendulum swinging the other way. Unlike him, I'm a graduate of the "bias for action" school; I'd rather make a decision and get on with it. If new information comes in, I'm willing to listen and adjust accordingly.

One of the simplest but most effective ways that I put my bias for action into effect is to handle each piece of paper that comes across my desk only once. As promised by time management gurus, this small act of self-discipline has amazing effects. Not only does it keep the avalanche of paper that comes into my office somewhat under control, the daily practice keeps me in training for decision-making on a larger scale.

The second rule for decision-making, I think, is to do your homework. Remember our travel agency and security businesses? Our organizational decision-making skills definitely improved in quality after we put more muscle into disciplined study. I don't think we would have been able to diversify successfully into the limited-service lodging market, for example, had we not devoted so much energy to studying the competition thoroughly in order to design Courtyard by Marriott.

On the flip side, study needs to come to an end at some point and a choice must be made. Don't let dotting *i*'s and crossing *t*'s become a convenient way to avoid following the first rule: *Make* a decision.

If this caveat sounds contradictory coming from someone who earlier in this book made such a fuss about Marriott's obsession with detail, allow me to clarify. I think a lot of executives—my father among them—use minute analysis as a way to cope with the fear of making a decision. If you're someone who suffers from analysis paralysis, you know what I'm talking about. More often than not, the critical information needed to make an informed decision does not require delving into microscopic details. To use Courtyard as an example again, we studied the competition to a fare-thee-well in order to *design* the product; the *decision* to go after the market was made long before we got into convening focus groups, constructing potential room layouts, etc.

The truth is, when it comes to making decisions, doing your homework only gets you so far. Which brings me to my third rule of decision-making: Listen to your heart. Research and analysis should give you the hard data you need to debate a decision with intelligence and insight, but facts alone aren't always enough to make a correct decision.

Heart is not "winging it." It is experience speaking. Nothing—not even number-crunching at its best—can take the place of cumulative, hands-on knowledge. That's because the central ingredients of heart are your understanding of and experience with your business. They're legitimate, if not vital, factors in making a decision.

I'll give you just two examples from Marriott's past to illustrate my point. One decision was made virtually overnight. The other involved more than two years of careful study. In the end, heart was the true deciding factor in each case.

In February 1995, Jim Sullivan, one of our senior development executives, was meeting with Fred

Malek, former head of Marriott's Lodging Group, for one of the pair's periodic "What's up with you?" chats. As Jim was heading out the door at the end, Fred casually asked: "Oh, by the way, you wouldn't be interested in Ritz-Carlton, would you?" Jim quickly closed the door, sat back down, and on April 25, less than three months later, Marriott and Ritz-Carlton closed a deal to bring Ritz-Carlton into the Marriott family.

The determination to acquire a major interest in the management of Ritz-Carlton's thirty-one hotels was probably the quickest major decision that we have ever made. We had been thinking about getting into the luxury tier of lodging, so the opportunity was right on target. We know the hotel business, we were very familiar with the Ritz product and its great market appeal, and we could see clearly that the fit would be a good one. The number-crunching before the paper-work was signed was important, but it was definitely not the deciding factor. Heart was.

The second example of heart in action involved a two-year debate in the early 1980s over whether or not Marriott should acquire Disney. Our flirtation with the idea is probably the company's most dramatic example of a well-studied fork in the road. One former Marriott executive who was a pivotal figure in exploring the Disney possibility believes it's one of the most significant "roads not taken" in American business history.

His characterization is too grand, but Disney does definitely rank as a defining moment for Marriott. When we were looking into acquiring the company, Walt Disney's original empire had been treading water for a number of years. Walt had died in 1966, and it seemed to many observers that the creative spark of the company had died with him. The Disney organization was ripe for revitalization.

I was attracted to the idea of acquiring Disney because of the company's legendary success with Disneyland and Disney World and, naturally, the hotels associated with the parks. It seemed to me that the combination of the Marriott brand with the Disney brand could have been phenomenal. Both organizations are family-oriented and share clean-cut values. Each had had charismatic founders who forged strong corporate cultures. Together, we might have dominated the family and leisure travel markets.

The idea of acquiring Disney had plenty to recommend it, but—unlike Ritz-Carlton—it was not a decision that could be made in the blink of an eye. For one thing, Disney was larger than Marriott. We'd have had to borrow $2.5 billion to bankroll the acquisition. Even in the big-deal days of the 1980s, that kind of money would have been a bet-the-ranch transaction for our company. And there was a good chance that Disney wasn't going to welcome our interest. Disney also consisted of more than hotels; we would be taking on the crème de la crème of theme parks, plus a film business about which we knew absolutely nothing.

We quietly studied Disney, trying to get a feel for not only the numbers, but the culture and traditions of the company. The Disney organization was known for being pretty tight-lipped about its internal workings. We even approached Disney to do a small hotel deal to get our foot in the door, meet the key players, and get some firsthand experience with the company.

For more than two years, we scrutinized Disney—coming as close as I've ever experienced to a case of analysis paralysis on my watch—until we knew the company almost as well as we knew ourselves. In the end, it came down to exactly that: knowing our strengths and weaknesses well enough to have a strong feeling that the acquisition simply was not right for Marriott.

What precisely did my heart tell me? For one thing, too much of Disney's success and intrinsic value rested on a creative spark that I didn't feel we had. I knew that we would not be comfortable trying to run a business—especially one larger than Marriott—that depended upon a steady stream of creative juices focused on entertainment to make it work. At the time, we had learned this lesson in our own Great America theme parks. I couldn't, at that moment, foresee finding anyone to take over Disney and provide it with the imaginative leadership that I knew the company needed to reach its potential. It was too risky to acquire Disney if we couldn't make it extremely successful.

At one point, we looked into the possibility of asking someone else to buy Disney's movie division, leaving Marriott with the parks and hotels. Although Disney's film business in the early 1980s was small compared to what it is today, it was one of the key points of the company that I personally didn't feel comfortable with. We suggested to Coca-Cola that they take a look at the film side; they owned Columbia Pictures Industries Inc., and former baseball commissioner Fay Vincent was running it as president and CEO. Marriott's chief financial officer, Gary Wilson, and Vincent talked it over during a flight aboard Coca-Cola's corporate jet. Vincent gave it some thought and made a midair decision: No thanks. Columbia was providing enough challenges at the time, and another film venture didn't sound appealing. Not long after that, I decided to let the opportunity go.

The upshot is that Michael Eisner soon came along and helped catapult Disney back into the forefront of the entertainment business. Today, as everyone knows, the Disney empire is wildly successful.

Eisner once asked me why I decided not to buy Disney. I told him it was because I didn't know someone like him existed. If I'd been aware that a leader with his creative talent was available to run the show, I might have made a different decision.

The reality is, I *probably* still would have said no. My personal desire to be hands-on would have prevented me from giving even someone as talented as Eisner the run of the place—which is what would have been required to make the acquisition a success. I would also have been constantly worried about Disney's size and complexity siphoning my attention away from Marriott's original businesses. I would not have been happy to make that sacrifice.

We made the right decision about Disney based on what we knew and what my heart told me at the time. I won't deny that the high financial stakes were part of the decision—the price tag of Disney would have exceeded Marriott's total annual sales at the time— but ultimately I made the choice based on knowing my own limits. The fact that it took us nearly three years to reach a definitive decision itself tells me that we probably made the correct choice. If Disney had been right for us, it would not have taken us so long to see it.

The Disney question is a fine example of an opportunity that came and went, never to return. It's also a good illustration of what I think is the fourth rule of decision-making: Don't waste time regretting, revisiting, or ruminating over what might have been.

Have there been moments when I've wondered what might have happened if Marriott had acquired Disney? Sure. But I made peace with the decision years ago. The making peace part is important in decision-making. If you spend time going over the what if's of every decision you make, you do nothing but waste time that could otherwise be going into exploring new opportunities.

Occasionally, circumstances change so dramatically that it's appropriate to take another look at an opportunity from a fresh perspective. When we turned down the chance to buy John Portman's original Atlanta hotel in 1965, for example, it was the right decision for Marriott at the time. At that stage in Marriott's evolution as a hotel company, we weren't ready to appreciate the cutting-edge architecture of a John Portman. We were still focused on getting those all-important basics in place and opening our first downtown hotel.

Twenty years later, the story was different. By then, we were at a point in our development that having a couple of Portman-designed properties in our portfolio was the right fit and gave us a nice halo. Times Square in New York City was the site of one of the two Marriott Marquis hotels that Portman put together for us. The other is the Marriott Marquis in—yes—Atlanta. There was something especially appropriate about having Atlanta be the site of one of Portman's designs for us.

We haven't only revisited decisions about individual properties. We've also taken another look at broad philosophical issues when the timing has been right. Hotel franchising is the example that comes to mind first. I've already touched upon Marriott's earliest— and ambivalent—experiences with hotel franchising. We reefed our sails after our Marriott Inn franchise program failed to flourish in the 1960s. Among other things, our corporate culture just wasn't ready to embrace the idea of being a franchiser organization.

By the early 1990s, when we needed to jump-start growth after a couple of years of licking our wounds, our attitude toward franchising was much more open-minded. We came back to the issue with a different viewpoint, different needs, and different goals. Hence, our decision was different. We're still adjusting to the role of franchiser, but this time we've put our heart where our policy is.

Another area where we try to put heart into policy is the arena of gambling. Beginning in the late 1970s and early 1980s, many lodging chains began to turn their attention to legalized gambling. It's a lucrative business and, in the eyes of some, a glamorous one.

We opted not to follow the pack. The pros and cons of getting into gambling (or gaming, as some call it) were pretty straightforward for us. The main argument on the side of entering the business is the power of the established Marriott name. We were virtually assured of success if we opted to build casino hotels.

In my mind, however, the negatives readily outweighed the positives, and still do today. For one thing, the gambling and lodging businesses are completely different; the two might often be found in one building, but their operations—right down to the way their books are kept—have little in common. The result, I think, is that one has to give way to the other. I've watched many Marriott competitors go so far down the road into gambling that their original business—lodging—has become a secondary thought. Their attention has been diverted away from what was once their core business. Given our presence in and love of lodging, I couldn't see allowing the company to be pulled in a direction that would do short shrift to what we do best.

Frankly, too, the culture of Marriott—I keep coming back to the culture of the company—simply doesn't fit comfortably with what I've seen of the gambling trade. Our overall business is basically a family-oriented enterprise. We take pride in that image. And I am personally uncomfortable with what I perceive to be the negative effects of gambling.

Some would argue that if gambling is lucrative as a business, Marriott as a public company has an obligation to pursue it. I strongly disagree. Corporate leaders all across the country make decisions every day about which businesses to get into or out of. And not all of those decisions are based on economics.

Is our decision about gambling written in stone? No. Like any rule, there are exceptions. Today, we have a half dozen casinos in Marriott hotels overseas, largely to meet local market conditions. Here in the United States, if one of our key urban markets legalized gambling and all of our competitors leaped in, we'd be forced to revisit the decision to remain competitive. But I can guarantee that we would be very careful about how we'd go about it.

Above all, I know we would use the four key steps I've outlined earlier to help us make what I hope would be the *right* decision for *us*.

12

DECIDE TO DECIDE

The unfortunate thing about this world is that good habits are so much easier to give up than bad ones.

—SOMERSET MAUGHAM

A few minutes before ten on the morning of October 2, 1989, I hurried aboard an Amtrak train at Union Station in Washington, D.C., for a three-hour trip to New York City. The miserable rain outside mirrored my lousy mood. I had been awakened by chest pains in the middle of the night and had not been able to go back to sleep. Instead, I'd gotten up, popped a couple of aspirins, pedaled my stationary bike for a few minutes, and headed to the office before 6:00 A.M.

As I settled into my seat for the long ride, I still wasn't feeling up to snuff.

Two minutes before we were due to pull out of the station, I grabbed my briefcase and hopped off the car, my chest on fire. Bracey, my driver, had stuck around, in case I didn't make the train. I jumped into the backseat, and he raced to Georgetown University Hospital.

The episode at Union Station was just the beginning. Over the course of the next three months, I suffered two more heart attacks and underwent a coronary bypass operation. Counting time in the hospital and time at home recuperating, I was out of commission for the better part of six months.

■

When you're going through something like a heart attack, you tend to think that a mistake of gigantic proportions has just been made. Someone else—not *you*, never *you*—is supposed to be lying in this particular hospital bed, staring at the ceiling or watching an IV drip.

In my case, there was no mistake; I was exactly where my bad habits had put me. For years leading up to my heart attacks, I had been the walking stereotype of the workaholic executive: too little exercise and rest, too much work, and too many heavy dinners too late at night. By the third heart attack, I concluded that if cardiovascular trouble didn't kill me, my wife, Donna, probably would if I didn't make some changes in the way I was living.

Most of the adjustments I made were the standard, commonsensical ones we've all heard about. I changed my diet, cut back on travel a little bit, began exercising more regularly, and picked our lakeside home in New Hampshire as the relaxing place to visualize when I need to calm down during stressful moments.

The most difficult change by far was attitudinal. Not only did I inherit my father's workaholism and heart problems, I also picked up his habit of worrying.

While Dad was alive, he frequently handwrote long notes to me in the dead of night because he literally couldn't rest until he'd gotten whatever was bothering him on paper. Night-shift associates at our properties would do a double-take when they spotted the chairman walking briskly through a hotel kitchen at 3:00 A.M. Dad paid for his perpetual restlessness with an ongoing series of illnesses that sometimes took him away from the office for months at a time. My mother spent a great portion of her time nursing him back to health, only to watch him lose it again to work and worry.

I've never been quite as bad as my father about getting a decent night's sleep. On the other hand, I probably didn't learn as much as I should have from his up-and-down state of health. Or at least I didn't learn until I got waylaid by serious illness myself. Like Dad, I have a hard time sitting still when there's work to be done. (And there's *always* work to be done.) I definitely have a rough time not worrying about the millions of things large and small that can go wrong at Marriott.

The irony, of course, is that my heart attacks only brought *more* worries. One of the worst aspects of the illness was the timing. In the fall of 1989, some of the signs of bad economic times that I've mentioned earlier were becoming hard to ignore. It didn't speed my recovery being upset by the unpleasant thought that I was sidelined just as we were perhaps about to encounter some of our biggest challenges. It was not easy to face the fact that three decades of sixteen-hour days on the job had put me in the very position I most wanted to avoid: not being at the helm if we hit rough seas.

Rough seas or not, my body told me in no uncertain terms that I had to slow down, take it easier, and make some fundamental attitude changes—or risk getting socked again with another heart attack.

One key attitude adjustment I made in the aftermath of illness was to become better at delegation. I still chomp at the bit waiting for results from our team, but I no longer feel compelled to have my hands in everything that goes on in the company. Don't get me wrong. My penchant for being hands-on remains as strong as ever; I simply don't exercise it twenty-four hours a day. (Donna would probably say I've cut back to twenty-three and a half.) Probably the most important sign of my attitude about delegation was the decision in February 1997 to place the presidency of Marriott International in the hands of Bill Shaw, a twenty-two-year veteran of the company and one of our most admired and trusted executives.

In addition to cutting back on the quantity of work I personally handle, I'm also working harder at saying no to demands on my time. It's not easy. I have a strong inclination for listening to a wide variety of viewpoints; it's difficult to acknowledge that I simply can't afford to make time for everyone who wants to discuss an issue with me. Naturally, my time with family and Marriott associates takes precedence. Time for my church activities remains a high priority, as do my duties on various boards of directors, but invitations to just about everything else are frequently politely turned down. Saying no is hard for me, but it has to be.

One of the most valuable lessons that my heart attacks taught me is to improve the balance in my life between work and play. If this sounds like an odd goal to which to aspire, you've probably never suffered from chronic workaholism. My vision of a perfect vacation includes sitting in the sunshine on my dock in New Hampshire, watching speedboats career past me while I chat on the telephone nonstop with a parade of people in the field and at headquarters. If you think I'm kidding, ask my secretary, Phyllis, or any member of my family. I'm *trying* to be better about leaving the office behind on weekends and on vacation. It's one lifelong habit that I don't really expect to lick, but I'm giving it my best shot. I've learned my lesson—at least in theory—about the high price of working too hard.

While lying on my back in the hospital, I learned something else. Marriott the man might be felled by illness, but Marriott the company has a constitution of iron. Our executive team stepped up to the challenge of my illness beautifully. Evidence of our company's ability to weather my sudden incapacitation made a significant dent in my anxiety about not being in the office. Remember what I said earlier about not letting an institution be held hostage by the presence or absence of a single individual? I'd have been devastated if our sixtysome-year-old company had fallen into disarray or paralysis simply because I was out of commission for a few months. As much as anyone likes to think he or she is indispensable, it was gratifying and comforting to see Marriott's organizational maturity and teamwork come through in what could have been a crisis.

Why have I told you all this? If even one person learns from my negative experience, changes his or her habits, and is spared a heart attack or other serious illness, I'll be pleased. Anyone who thinks that pushing the limits of human endurance is necessary to a company's success should think again. My heart attacks merely made everyone worry, from family to friends to employees to Wall Street. Work hard by all means, but don't run up a huge tab of stress and worry. Sooner or later, you will pay for it, and so will everyone around you.

■

The other personal lesson that I want to share briefly is one that came early in my adult life and fortunately didn't require the drama of a heart attack to sink in. I learned the lesson growing up in my church, the Church of Jesus Christ of Latter-day Saints, also known as the Mormon Church. Former church president Spencer W. Kimball termed it "deciding to decide."

What does "deciding to decide" mean? For me, it meant that as a young man I concluded that I simply wouldn't do certain things like being unfaithful, smoking, drinking alcohol, or using drugs. I chose to put my family first, then my church, then my business. And I *decided* that that would be the last time I'd have to make a *decision* about those temptations or priorities.

Why have I highlighted "deciding to decide" when I've already talked about decision-making several times in this book? Because the kind of decision-making I'm talking about here is very personal. Like changing lifelong bad habits to prevent a heart attack, deciding to decide has ramifications that go well beyond the nine-to-five world to profoundly affect health, home, and family. I think it's worth the spotlight on its own.

Nineteenth-century philosopher Thomas Carlyle once said: "A man lives by believing something, not by debating and arguing about many things." Once you decide to decide, life becomes surprisingly simple. You don't have to think about certain issues or questions again. You simply get on with things and don't waste time and energy rehashing—debating and arguing—the problems and possibilities.

Probably the best analogy from Marriott's corporate culture is our attention to management systems. Once these basic systems are in place, you don't have to think about them anymore. When you decide to decide, you're not starting from scratch each time you're faced with a temptation or issue. You've got your answer at the ready.

Speaking purely from my own experience, a decision to make family a top priority, for example, can be tremendously gratifying. My happiest moments are those spent with my wife, Donna, our children, and our grandchildren. Mormons believe that families stay together for eternity, so we tend to view the family circle as the central source of daily support in our lives, in good times and bad. We laugh together, pray together, and give each other a boost when we're down.

In our family's case, togetherness extends to the workplace. My two oldest sons—Steve and John—and our son-in-law, Ron, have made the company a career. Our youngest son, David, plans to join the firm when he graduates from college. Working together is a pleasure, because we share a common vision and core personal values.

Deciding to decide and then sticking to those decisions has another benefit. Perhaps I sound old-fashioned, but I think there's satisfaction to be had in standing firm against the onslaught of temptations that come with contemporary life. Saying no consistently can give a sense of real power in a world that often seems out of control.

Both lessons I've touched on in this chapter have to do with recognizing personal limits. In the case of my heart attack, I learned that the old saying about robbing Peter to pay Paul has dangerous consequences. I stole from my health in order to satisfy my workaholic habits. For my trouble, I almost got to pay a premature visit to Saint Peter in Heaven.

In terms of making personal decisions and living up to them, deciding to decide is really nothing more than recognizing (and accepting) that there's only so much a human being can do or handle intelligently. Not everyone finds the idea of hard-and-fast choices easy to accept, but I've found it liberating. It can also keep you humble by providing an ongoing reminder that no one's judgment is so infallible that signposts and rules aren't necessary.

Both lessons are also about aspiring to something that I've talked about again and again in this book, something that perhaps best sums up the main challenge that each of us faces every day, at work, at home, at play: achieving *balance*.

No company, institution, or individual is likely to actually *find* the perfect balance. But in searching for it, you might just discover talents you didn't know you possessed, strength you never imagined, and a dream worth spending a lifetime to build.

I certainly have.

I have made mistakes, but I have never made the mistake of claiming that I never made one.

—JAMES GORDON BENNETT

AFTERWORD

An institution is the lengthened shadow of one man.

—Ralph Waldo Emerson

A few days after Bill Marriott hired me to work with him on this book, I got a call from his office asking if I was available to join a small group accompanying Bill on a two-day property tour in California the next week. I said yes, of course. In the short time that I'd been acquainted with the company, I knew that Bill's hands-on visits to Marriott's hotels were central to his management philosophy, not to mention legendary in their intensity. Seeing him in action would be the perfect way to kick off our working relationship.

I flew out to Los Angeles the night before our tour was to begin. Bill was due at the LAX Marriott the next morning at 8:00 A.M. About an hour ahead of time, I rode down the elevator for a quick trip to the hotel's gift shop. Staff were all busy at their usual jobs, but I could detect a special energy in the air: "Mr. Marriott" was coming for a visit.

Ten minutes early—no surprise, he hates being late—Bill arrived and the day began. For the next fourteen hours, we were in constant, measured motion. Seven hotels, 400 handshakes, dozens of pictures, 100 miles of freeway driving, and two meals later, the day's entourage finally parted ways. The next morning, we started all over again. Bill launched the day with a pep talk to one of Marriott's business councils, followed by visits to another half dozen properties, and finished up by boarding a flight to Arizona at the Orange County airport. As we pulled up to the building's entrance ten minutes before flight time, he was greeted by a group of excited Marriott associates from a hotel we had visited earlier in the day. Somehow, they had missed seeing him while he was at the property. There on the sidewalk, Bill shook everyone's hand enthusiastically and gathered the group around him for a couple of photos before dashing off to catch his plane.

I was impressed. I was also ready to collapse. My role on the trip, I'm almost ashamed to say, had been a tiny one: All I'd had to do was keep up with Bill and keep my hands out to accept the bags and boxes of cookies and other goodies that almost every property wanted to send along with us. Bill had been the focal point of nonstop attention, from dawn to well past dusk, for two solid days.

"Don't you ever get tired of this?" I asked him at one point toward the end of the first day, while we stood alone waiting for an elevator. He rolled his eyes. "I've been doing this all my life. I wouldn't know how to *stop*, even if I wanted to."

What he didn't say, but that soon became very clear to me, is that Bill *doesn't* want to stop.

Why should he when the effect he has on Marriott associates in the field is almost magical? During our two days on the road, GM after GM pulled me aside to tell me that their staff "would be high on this visit for months to come." Bill himself would be far too modest to characterize it this way, but a visit from the person he calls "a guy named Marriott" is like a visit from royalty.

Just watching the expressions on the faces of staff as he works his way through every nook and cranny of a hotel is evidence enough. The reactions range from smiling embarrassment to backslapping affection. Bill does his best to break any ice with a kindliness and gentle enthusiasm calibrated to put people at ease. No one escapes his attention; he makes a point of shaking the hand of even the shyest associate hiding in a corner of the kitchen.

From what I witnessed, property tours are definitely not make-nice cakewalks or cynical photo ops. Bill really does check out closets, bathrooms, kitchens, and storerooms. Watching a distinguished man in a well-pressed suit surrounded by an entourage of executives check under a bed takes a little getting used to. But nothing is beneath Bill's notice. A bedspread that's too short or long, a mirror hung crookedly, a scratched coffee table, a worn carpet, and cracked bathroom tiles are all noted and commented upon. The hotel's "numbers" likewise receive close inspection. Although Bill is quick to praise good work, GMs who haven't done their homework come in for the kind of long, disappointed look that students dread from a favorite teacher. While never for one moment ungracious, Bill also has a way of making clear when he thinks a GM is a little too self-satisfied for the Marriott Way. A wise GM takes note.

This would all be impressive enough if Bill were someone who thrived in the spotlight. But it's even more so because he considers himself to be a shy man. Happiness, he told me at one point, is an afternoon spent quietly on a sofa in his sunlit den reading military history or a biography. His social life focuses on his wife, Donna, and their four grown children and their families, punctuated by an occasional evening out to catch the latest action movie at a local theater. The only other regular activity besides business that takes Bill away from home is the fifteen to twenty hours of volunteer work he does each week for his church.

So why does this intensely private man put himself stage-center 100 days a year? Especially when personal wealth and a career that has already spanned four decades give him an easy out? Bill would probably say habit and workaholism, a case of not knowing "how to stop." Others, including his wife and children, would say a love of the business and a sense of duty to the company so deep that personal shyness readily gives way to both. Both answers are correct, but after a year of listening to all sides of the question, I'd put my money on the latter.

In every conversation, Bill's passion for the company that he has built shines through. He might be modest about his own evolution as an executive and leader of a major global corporation, but he's unabashedly proud of the Marriott organization. He also has faith enough in his company's track record and the soundness of its core philosophy to have sent me out on the road to hear Marriott critiqued frankly by dozens of current and former associates, including some who now work for competitors. Not every CEO has the courage to give a stranger carte blanche to delve into his or her organization's psyche . . . especially when that psyche is a direct reflection of the CEO.

By and large, of course, what I heard was positive. And why not? Anyone who can get an eye half open can see that Marriott *is* a great American business success story. The company isn't perfect—a fact which the people I talked to were uniformly quick to point out— but it certainly has done an awful lot of things right. One thing it has managed to do is inspire incredible loyalty. As I was being regaled with anecdotes about Marriott's "spirit to serve" and the company's other core values, I was struck by the intense sincerity of the speakers. I was also impressed by their candor. I've been a roving corporate historian long enough to recognize an official party line when I hear one. On this project, I was treated to affectionate but clear-eyed critical commentary in all but a handful of cases. Marriott appears to be a well-loved and respected institution, blemishes and all.

That's not to say that challenges to Marriott's honor go undefended. In an interview with one retired Marriott old-timer, I doggedly poked around trying to identify Bill's weak spots as a leader to help me gain a better understanding of him and the company. Playing devil's advocate, I ticked off a list of dubious decisions that the company had made over the years for which I wanted explanations. Answering each charge, the interviewee finally threw his hands up in the air in mock exasperation: "Give the man some credit! How many people do you know who are walking on water today, young lady?"

Once I assured the man that I really did *like* Bill, we parted good friends.

The interview with the crusty Marriott veteran was far from the only one to yield an interesting insight into the effect that Marriott—both man and company—have had over the years. One of the most revealing stories I heard bubbled up spontaneously at the end of a session with a former executive who left Marriott fifteen years ago to pursue a very lucrative career in investments. Told by anyone else, the anecdote would be easy to dismiss as too maudlin to be of value. This man, however, struck me as being a fairly unsentimental sort; the front hallway of his estate is dominated by a medieval suit of armor, an apt warning to all who enter. His comments about Marriott had been the most abrupt and blunt that I'd heard in my travels.

Ushering me safely past the visored iron soldier at

the close of our chat, he was on the verge of saying good-bye when his expression suddenly softened and he began recounting a story from his days as a young executive at Marriott. He had accompanied Bill on a property tour. While the group was gathered in one of the public spaces of a hotel, he observed the reaction of an associate across the room who suddenly recognized Bill. By the man's gait and demeanor, it was clear that he was learning disabled. The associate's eyes lit up, and he charged across the room toward Bill, his arms open wide. Not missing a beat, Bill threw open his own arms to meet the man's enthusiastic embrace.

Fifteen years later, standing in the driveway of his home, a lifetime and lifestyle removed from Marriott, the former executive was still struck by what he had seen next. Standing behind Bill, he noticed tears running down the cheeks of the associate.

Lovely as the story is, I know that it's not the only occasion on which Bill has inspired such a heartfelt reaction from a Marriott employee. What impressed me most about the incident was the fact that the former Marriott executive—almost without thinking about it—had felt compelled to share this particular memory. His previous forty-five minutes of tough words about Marriott seemed to melt away, replaced by a brief flicker of awe that a business leader could touch an employee's heart and life so directly.

In the months since that interview, I've had plenty of opportunities to hear about the many other ways in which Bill Marriott has influenced and shaped the lives of hundreds of thousands of Marriott associates. I've concluded that Ralph Waldo Emerson's observation about the "true test" of a country deserves another twist beyond what Bill gave it in his opening to Chapter 1.

To wit, the true test of a *leader* is the kind of *company* he turns out.

From what I've seen and heard of the Marriott enterprise during the past year, Bill Marriott passes the test with flying colors.

KATHI ANN BROWN
Arlington and Charlottesville, Virginia
September 1997

MARRIOTT MILESTONES

1927

J. Willard Marriott marries Alice Sheets and the couple moves to Washington, D.C., from Marriott Settlement, Utah. Hugh Colton and the Marriotts pool $3,000 each to finance an A&W franchise, root beer concentrate and restaurant equipment. On May 20, the company's first root beer stand opens at 3128 14th Street, N.W. Hot food is added later, and the name The Hot Shoppe is adopted. Colton sells out a year later for $5,000 and moves back to Utah.

1929

Hot Shoppes, Inc. is officially incorporated in the state of Delaware.

1932

J. Willard (Bill) Marriott, Jr., is born in Washington, D.C.

1934

Company opens a Hot Shoppe in Baltimore, Maryland—its first restaurant outside of Washington, D.C.

1937

Hot Shoppes pioneers airline catering at Hoover Field (current site of the Pentagon) in Washington, D.C. In-Flite catering division begins service to Eastern, American, and Capital airlines.

1939

Richard Marriott, younger brother of Bill, is born in Washington, D.C. Hot Shoppes launches food service management business with an account at the U.S. Treasury building.

1941–45

During World War II, Hot Shoppes feeds many of the thousands of workers who move to the nation's capital to work in defense plants and government complexes.

1946

Bill Marriott begins his first job with Hot Shoppes at age fourteen. His assignment: stapling invoices together for the accounting department. During his high school years, he works in the D.C. Hot Shoppes cooking burgers, washing dishes, and mopping floors.

1947

First industrial cafeterias run by Hot Shoppes open at the General Motors plant in Georgia and the Ford Motor plant in Virginia.

1953

Company stock first offered to public at $10.25 per share. Offering sells out in two hours of trading.

1954

Bill Marriott graduates from the University of Utah with a degree in banking and finance, followed by a two-year stint (1954–56) as a ship's supply officer aboard the U.S.S. *Randolph*. While in the Navy, he proposes—long distance—to Donna Garff, daughter of a professor at the University of Utah. Total annual sales for the company in 1954 reach $21.5 million.

1955

Ground is broken in Arlington, Virginia, for the company's first motor hotel: Twin Bridges. Plans call for 365 air-conditioned rooms equipped with telephone, radio, and television; a Hot Shoppe restaurant; barber shop; variety store; gasoline station; swimming pool and recreation area; and adjacent guest parking. One noteworthy feature is a drive-in registration desk "which will enable guests to register in their automobiles. Bicycle attendants will guide guests to their rooms." The project is billed in the annual report as: "The World's Largest Motor Hotel Owned and

Operated by Hot Shoppes, Inc. Combining Motel Convenience with Hotel Luxury." The same year, the company launches a highway food service division and begins serving food at Children's Hospital in Washington, D.C., its first hospital account, and at American University, its first education account. Corporate headquarters are consolidated at 5161 River Road, Washington, D.C. The site includes eleven acres, a test kitchen, a modern employee cafeteria, a print shop, and railroad sidings.

1956

Bill Marriott joins the company full-time. Sales exceed $29 million.

1957

Twin Bridges "motor hotel" opens in Arlington, Virginia. Bill Marriott takes over management of the company's lodging division. Company opens its first "Mighty Mo" curb-service restaurant. Total annual sales for the year exceed $36 million.

1958

The Hot Shoppes' second hotel—Key Bridge Marriott—is under construction. According to the company's annual report for 1958, the facility will have 210 rooms and is "ideally situated to accommodate tourists and businessmen visiting the city of Washington."

1959

Key Bridge Marriott opens. Two-year-old Debbie Marriott, Bill and Donna's daughter, snips the ribbon. Bill Marriott is named vice president, hotel operations. The company's first Sirloin & Saddle specialty restaurant opens in the Twin Bridges hotel: "The room features a Western atmosphere where the rough textures of the bricks, carpets, and wood paneling provide strong accents. It is interesting that the weathered oak paneling used for the walls is over 100 years old and was brought from our Fairfield Farm in the foothills of the Appalachian Mountains in Virginia." Sales have almost doubled since 1955 to $46 million.

1960

Third motor hotel—Dallas-Stemmons Marriott—opens. Marriott's hotel growth strategy focuses on targeting suburban locations near airports and major convention cities. Lodging division begins recruiting management teams. Ground is broken for a fourth hotel on Philadelphia's City Line Avenue. Company's profit sharing program begins. Total sales for the year exceed $54 million. Employees: 7,000.

1961

Fourth motor hotel—Philadelphia Marriott—opens. The facility's three restaurants include the company's first venture into luxury Polynesian food, the Kona Kai. In what will become a major financing strategy in subsequent years, three of the company's hotel properties are sold and leased back as a means of raising additional capital for growth. Annual report notes that the company is emphasizing "the most modern, professional management techniques." Total annual sales exceed $58 million. Employees: 8,600. Total units in all divisions—restaurants, flight kitchens, and hotels—reach 100.

1962

Main focus of company's lodging division is on adding major convention facilities, exhibit space, and rooms to existing hotels. Marriott continues to recruit veteran "hotel men" from other companies, including Hilton and Sheraton, to expand its lodging management team. The company successfully installs its first computer, an IBM 1401.

1963

Ground is broken for company's fifth hotel—the Atlanta Marriott—the first major new convention hotel in the city since 1930. The Hot Shoppes' In-Flite catering division is "one of the largest operations in the industry, serving twenty-five airlines at ten major airports." The company opens food service facilities at the Smithsonian Institution and the newly opened Dulles International Airport. Hot Shoppes reorganizes into six major operating divisions: service restaurants, cafeterias, motor hotels, airline catering, institutional food service, and manufacturing.

1964

Company changes its name to Marriott–Hot Shoppes, Inc. At age thirty-two, Bill Marriott is elected president and a member of the board of directors. Marriott announces debut of Hot Shoppes, Jr., in response to new fast-food trend. Company begins to receive inquiries about its willingness to manage hotels on a fee basis. Total annual sales exceed $84 million. Employees: 9,600.

1965

Fifth hotel—Atlanta Marriott—opens. Sixth and seventh Marriott hotels are in the planning stages.

Marriott's first fast-food restaurant, Hot Shoppes, Jr., boasting a "fifteen-cent hamburger," opens in suburban Washington, D.C.

1966

Sixth hotel—Saddlebrook, New Jersey, Marriott—opens. The six Marriott hotels check in more than 1 million guests during the year. The Hot Shoppes menu includes 385 items. Recipe card system introduced. In-Flite goes international with a flight kitchen in Caracas, Venezuela. Sales reach $123 million, a 25 percent increase over the previous year. On average, gains in sales have exceeded 15 percent annually. Employees: 12,500.

1967

In its fortieth anniversary year, Marriott–Hot Shoppes, Inc. renames itself Marriott Corporation. Company purchases the 22-unit Big Boy coffeeshop chain from founder Bob Wian. Marriott will eventually grow the chain to 120 company-owned units, principally in mid-Atlantic and Western states. Ground is broken for largest flight kitchen ever built, at JFK Airport in New York. Hotel construction is under way in Boston, Chicago (O'Hare), and Houston. Expansions under way at Philadelphia, Key Bridge, and Atlanta Marriott hotels. Company opens its first golf course at the Camelback Inn in Arizona. Operating units: 206.

1968

Marriott acquires Robee's fast-food chain and develops Roy Rogers brand name. Marriott Inn franchising program announced. Company acquires its first resort, the Camelback Inn in Scottsdale, Arizona. Marriott is listed on New York Stock Exchange for the first time. In-Flite division takes off internationally, while the Hot Shoppes division reaches its peak. Approximately 90 percent of company's sales come from food and beverage sales, and 10 percent from lodging. Employees: 19,700.

1969

Marriott enters international lodging market with a leased hotel (Paraiso) in Acapulco, Mexico. Company purchases major New York City hotel—Essex House. Ten Marriott hotels are now open. Company's architecture and construction division is touted as "unique in industry," assuring Marriott control over design quality. Total annual sales for the year exceed $257 million, $58 million of which comes from the lodging division. Marriott reorganizes and consolidates into three divisions: restaurant operations, In-Flite, and hotels.

1970

Sales for the year exceed $315 million. First franchised Marriott Inns open, mostly in Midwest cities. Twelve-story tower added to Key Bridge hotel. Operating units: 382. Employees: 26,000.

1971

Marriott's first Joshua Tree restaurant opens in McLean, Virginia. Hot Shoppes, Jr.—Marriott's entry into fast food—is struggling against proliferation of McDonald's and other chains. Diversification push begins. Marriott World Travel is established. First of a series of recession-plagued years. The annual report notes: "Marriott Hotels felt the sting of the sluggish economy most severely, and were unable to contribute as much to our profit growth as we had hoped." Sales: $347 million. Operating units: 419. Employees: 27,900.

1972

Marriott enters Sun Line cruise ship partnership and announces plans for two Great America theme parks. Acquires Farrell's ice cream parlor chain. The company now has eighteen hotels, twelve of which have been built in the past six years. Bill Marriott is named chief executive officer of Marriott Corporation. Total annual sales exceed $422 million, a 20 percent increase over previous year. Marriott's stock splits for the first time, two-for-one. Plans are announced for construction of first Marriott hotel in Europe, a 400-room property to be located in Amsterdam. Operating units: 508.

1973

First lodging management contracts are negotiated, marking the beginning of Marriott's evolution into a hotel *management* company. Company also acquires security business, the Hallmark Corporation, and renames it Marriott Security Systems. Restaurant division launches more specialty lines: Phineas Prime Rib and Franklin Stove. Marriott acquires Sam Lord's Castle, a well-known resort property in Barbados. Sun Line's third cruise ship, the *Stella Solaris*, makes her maiden voyage. Total annual sales reach $500 million.

1974

Future Marriott International president and COO William Shaw joins the company as an accounting manager. Economic recession of early 1970s continues, curtailing leisure and business travel. Company adds 118 units, bringing the total to 688, doubling

Marriott's restaurants, food service accounts, and In-Flite kitchens in just five years. Company serves 600,000 people each day in its restaurants, hotels, airline flights, and cruise ships. Construction gets under way for Great America theme parks in Santa Clara, California, and Gurnee, Illinois. Employees: 42,800.

1975

The Cypriot War ruins the first full season of Marriott's partnership in Sun Line cruise ships. Economic recession continues to hold down the company's hotel occupancy rates and restaurant profits. The company opens seven new hotels and fifty-two new restaurants, acquires a dozen more restaurants, but cancels six hotel projects and takes a $500 million write-off; the projects are "discontinued because their projected return failed to meet our criteria for profitability." Amsterdam Marriott opens. Marriott experiences its first earnings decline in fifteen years, thanks in part to recession, inflation, and Sun Line's losses.

1976

Marriott's two Great America parks open during Bicentennial year. Marriott Security Systems division is sold after only three years. Total sales reach $890 million, a 21 percent increase over previous year.

Marriott's hotels, resorts, and franchised inns together offer a total of 14,510 rooms. Marriott's In-Flite division is the largest independent caterer to airlines, serving 120 U.S. and foreign carriers. Employees: 60,600.

1977

Sales hit $1 billion during Marriott's fiftieth anniversary year. The company's financial philosophy changes, launching an era of debt financing that will fuel growth in the 1980s. Among other things, plans are underway to sell several of the company's early hotels and take back management contracts. Annual report announces that "soon, more than 50 percent of our hotel rooms are expected to be under management agreement." Company sets up strategic planning department and breaks ground for new corporate headquarters in Bethesda, Maryland.

1978

As part of its strategy to move away from hotel ownership to hotel management, Marriott has already sold more than half its room capacity to investors. Annual report for the year notes that the company's diversification efforts will focus on capital sources, not businesses. Announces 20/20 financial goals: 20 percent return on equity, 20 percent growth in sales. Architecture and Construction (A&C) division completes $100 million in construction in a single year. Hotels are the company's "most rapidly growing group." Marriott hotels are now operating in forty-six cities.

1979

The company sells Marriott World Travel and company's dinner house division. Both moves fit with company's announcement in 1977 that its focus will be on growing the lodging division. Total annual sales increase by $500 million in just two years to $1.5 billion. By the end of 1979, fifty hotels are in various stages of construction. Marriott begins repurchases of stock and sells off $90 million in "idle or marginally profitable assets." The decade's high inflation rates help fuel profits in room rates. Employees: 65,700.

1980

Planning begins on Courtyard by Marriott, the company's first entry into the moderate-priced lodging market. About 70 percent of all Marriott guest rooms are now owned by investors. Plans for the 1980s call for a 20 to 25 percent annual increase in guest rooms. Hotels begin to dominate company's overall sales, accounting for more than half. Nearly 100 hotels are in the A&C pipeline, twice the projection made in 1979. Annual report notes that "our goal throughout the 1980s will be to average 20 percent annual earnings growth, to increase dividends commensurate with this growth, and to maintain ROE [return on equity] in excess of 20 percent." In a major tender offer, the company buys back nearly one-fourth of its outstanding common stock. Between 1980 and 1989 the company's stock will leap in market value from $700 million to $3.5 billion.

1981

One hundredth hotel opens—Maui Marriott Resort, Hawaii. Marriott's annual sales surpass $2 billion, doubling in less than five years. Company arranges first limited partnership to finance eleven hotels by a syndicate of commercial banks. The lodging division sees a 40 percent increase in rooms in one year—the system now has 40,000 rooms in seventy-four cities. The annual report notes that Marriott is one of the "world's largest real estate developers, creating about $1 billion of product annually." Marriott's restaurant division continues streamlining and narrows its focus to expanding Roy Rogers (fast food) and Big Boy (coffeeshops). Employees: 81,800.

1982

Marriott estimates that its employees handle 6 million customer contacts each day. Gino's fast-food chain is acquired for conversion to Roy Rogers. In-Flite division receives big boost with acquisition of Host International, an eighty-five-year-old food service company with a specialty in airport concession operations. Marriott sells Farrell's ice cream parlors. The lodging division reaches $1 billion in annual sales for the first time. More than three-fourths of all Marriott guest rooms are owned by investors. Company has added 23,000 rooms in past year, bringing its total to 63,000 rooms in 118 hotels. An average of one Marriott hotel opens every two weeks. Lodging expansion plans "will enable Marriott to become the world's largest manager—as distinct from franchiser—of hotels." Approximately 70 percent of the company's sales are still in food and beverages. The company is expanding at an average rate of 20 percent annually.

1983

First Courtyard by Marriott opens outside of Atlanta, Georgia, surprising the moderate-priced lodging market and setting off an industrywide scramble to introduce new products. Marriott Honored Guest Awards frequent-stay program is established to build brand loyalty. The company now has 55,000 guest rooms in 133 hotels in seventy-nine cities. A total of 80,000 rooms is projected for the end of 1986. Ground is broken for two Marriott Marquis hotels designed by John Portman. Marriott bows out of the theme park business with the sale of both of its Great America theme parks. The 500th Roy Rogers opens. Employees: 109,000.

1984

Company's flagship, the JW Marriott Hotel, opens in Washington, D.C. After successful debut of Courtyard, Marriott quickly unveils other segmentation plans. Marriott Suites is announced; others will follow. Company acquires American Resorts Group. "Halo" hotel properties are acquired in Paris (Prince de Galles) and London (London Marriott). Company announces plans to grow to 100,000 rooms by 1990 (a goal achieved by 1987). Plans for first senior life-care community announced to open in 1987. Restaurant division continues to streamline by sale of the company's Mexican restaurants and more dinner houses. Marriott agrees to sell Essex House to Japanese investors, an early sign of fast-growing Japanese interest in American real estate. Total annual sales reach $3.5 billion. Marriott's sales and profits have doubled since 1980 and increased tenfold since 1971. Lodging now accounts for nearly half of the company's total sales. Marriott's hotels receive more Mobil Four- and Five-Star and AAA Four- and Five-Star awards than any other lodging chain.

1985

Marriott acquires Gladieux Corporation and Service Systems Corporation; the acquisitions transform Marriott into one of the three largest American companies in contract food service management. Company also acquires the Howard Johnson concern; under the deal, the hotels are sold to Prime Motor Inn and restaurants are kept for conversion to Big Boys. Marriott now has 149 full-service hotels and a total of 67,000 rooms. In what will prove to be an overly optimistic projection, Marriott announces that it should reach $10 billion in annual sales by the early 1990s. (Goal is eventually reached in 1996.) J. Willard Marriott dies at age eighty-four. One month later, Bill Marriott is elected as chairman of the board.

1986

Marriott acquires Saga Corporation, a major institutional food service and restaurant company. In-Flite has ninety-four kitchens serving more than 150 air-lines. Company announces plans for Fairfield Inn, an economy "rooms-only" product. Marriott's Orlando World Center opens, a 1,500-room convention facility that is the largest of its kind. Courtyard by Marriott opens twenty-five hotels, for a total of thirty-six; plans call for adding fifty to sixty annually. Company's stock splits five-for-one. Marriott is rated the number-one hotel company by *Business Travel News*.

1987

Marriott achieves its goal of 100,000 guest rooms three years ahead of schedule. Company acquires extended-stay Residence Inn chain and opens first Fairfield Inns and Marriott Suites. Lodging system now includes 361 properties. Marriott sells Big Boy franchise rights in anticipation of transforming the company's restaurants into a new chain dubbed Allie's, named after cofounder Alice Marriott. The company exits Sun Line cruise ships after fifteen years. Company's contract food services division contributes $2.9 billion, lodging $2.6 billion, and restaurants $879 million to the company's annual sales. Company serves nearly 5 million meals each day. Operating units: almost 4,000 in fifty states and twenty-four countries. Employees: 210,000.

1988

The majority of Marriott's 451 hotels are now in the limited-service segment, a major philosophical change for a company identified with full-service lodging for twenty-five years. The lodging division contributes 43 percent of total annual sales. Marriott itself owns only one out of every ten rooms under the Marriott flag. A&C division develops $1.4 billion of hotels this year. Backlog of unsold hotels begins to build as sluggishness in real estate market sets in. In spite of Marriott's growing public identification with lodging, the company still owns 1,100 restaurants in twenty-three states. Food and beverage sales in all divisions of the company account for almost three-quarters of the company's annual revenues. Allie's restaurant is unveiled on limited basis, but will not roll out on national basis as originally planned. ROE hits 30.4 percent for the year. Total annual sales: $7.3 billion. Senior Living Services division acquires Basic American Retirement Communities as part of growth strategy for 1990s. SLS announces plans to develop an assisted living concept to be called Brighton Gardens.

1989

Five hundredth hotel opens in Warsaw, Poland. Marriott's lodging system now includes 134,000 rooms in 539 hotels. Eighty-eight hotels added in 1989 alone. First Marriott hotel limited partnership sold to Japanese investors. The company's long-term debt stands at $3.3 billion—a record—as the company's backlog of hotel properties and the state of the American hotel industry begin to worry Wall Street. During a major corporate restructuring, Marriott sells off its restaurant and In-Flite divisions in a historic move that cuts the company loose from its original roots. The company acquires United Healthserve, a provider of housekeeping, maintenance, and laundry services and opens its first life-care retirement communities—the Quadrangle in Haverford, Pennsylvania, and the Fairfax in Alexandria, Virginia. Marriott's workforce stands at 229,000, an all-time high that will drop when company splits in 1992. Bill Marriott suffers three heart attacks between October and December.

1990

Economic trouble looming at year's end. Marriott adds 100 hotels—a rate of two new properties a week. Approximately fifty-seven new properties are scheduled to open in 1991, adding 16,000 rooms to the system. Nikkei index loses 40 percent value between January and October, causing Japanese investors to withdraw from American real estate market. Tensions in Middle East begin building toward the war that will erupt in January 1991. Marriott turns off hotel development pipeline as the U.S. real estate market crashes. The company's bonds are downgraded, but remain investment quality. Hotel franchising is mentioned for the first time as a major growth vehicle for the company. Marriott's A&C department is dismantled and more than 1,000 people are laid off. In cost-cutting move, capital expenditures will plummet from $1.2 billion to $427 million in 1991. The company institutes a salary freeze for the year, using a graduated timetable and weighting the burden toward senior staff.

1991

Marriott emphasizes in its annual report that it does "not intend to sacrifice value" by selling its backlog of hotels "at low prices to expedite transactions." Company announces that the lodging division will focus on franchising, conversions, and international markets for future growth. Leveraging of brand names ("branding") will also be a platform for expansion. Customer-service program First Ten is introduced at fourteen hotels. Marriott offers 59 million room nights a year. Company reduces its long-term debt level from a high of $3.6 billion to $2.9 billion.

1992

Marriott announces intention to split into two companies. Host Marriott will retain company-owned hotels and most of company's long-term debt; Marriott International (MI) will become a management services company. Bondholders react angrily; lawsuits are eventually settled. The two companies will maintain separate boards of directors and other administrative systems. Bill Marriott is slated to become president, CEO, and chairman of Marriott International. His younger brother, Richard Marriott, will become chairman of Host Marriott. Major reorganization under split places William Tiefel as president of Marriott Lodging Group and William Shaw as president of Marriott Services Group. Total annual sales reach $8.7 billion. Lodging now contributes 52 percent to the company's yearly sales. Marriott sells several full-service hotels and a group of Courtyard hotels in a drive to raise cash to pay down debt. Company acquires Dobbs airport concessions business, which will become part of Host Marriott Corporation after the split.

1993

Company split becomes official on October 5. Marriott settles suits with bondholders. Marriott International's lodging division reorganizes, consolidates, and streamlines itself along brand lines—a natural outgrowth of the company's decade-old segmentation drive. Nonlodging management services account for just under half of MI's sales. Marriott hotels total 784 in the United States and twenty-two other countries. Total annual sales for MI are $8 billion—up from $7.7 billion—after adjusting for split. MI employees: 170,000.

1994

Back in growth mode once again, Marriott International outlines plan to add 100,000 guest rooms by 1999, two-thirds in limited service and one-third in full service. According to annual report, Marriott manages 7 percent of all hotel rooms in North America and 2 percent in the world, giving the company "substantial growth opportunities." Franchising will be a "key driver of room growth" in the limited-service category. International lodging also becomes a special focus of the company's growth strategy. The Marriott Honored Guest Awards program is once again named best in the industry.

1995

One thousandth hotel opens in Kauai, Hawaii. Marriott International acquires a 49 percent interest in the Ritz-Carlton chain, with option to purchase remaining interest, after whirlwind three-month "courtship." Host Marriott announces plans to spin off Host Marriott Services Corporation, including Marriott's toll road, airport, and stadium concession businesses. Host Marriott will retain hotels and real estate. MI acquires Taylorplan Services, gaining access to the European management services market. Total annual sales for MI reach almost $9 billion, $5.3 billion contributed by lodging and $3.6 billion contributed by management services.

1996

Marriott International's Senior Living Services division acquires the Forum Group, which brings into the company forty-two senior living communities in nine states and doubles Marriott's presence in this industry. Fairfield Suites and TownePlace Suites by Marriott are announced. Britain's Whitbread hotels become Marriott hotel franchisees. Total guest rooms: 229,000 with 40,000 more in the pipeline. MI's Contract Services Group acquires Russell & Brand, Ltd., a UK-based food service company. Operating units: 4,700. Total annual sales for Marriott International top $10 billion for the first time. Company is the sixteenth largest employer in the United States. Employees: 192,000.

1997

Bill Shaw, a twenty-two-year veteran of the company and former head of MI's Contract Services Group, is named president and chief operating officer of Marriott International. Bill Marriott retains the positions of CEO and chairman of the board. MI rolls out its new Marriott Rewards program, the largest frequent-stay program in the industry, allowing guests to earn points to redeem at any of Marriott's lodging brands. Company also announces new lodging brand, Marriott Executive Residences. MI acquires the Renaissance Hotel Group for $1 billion. The acquisition adds three established lodging brands (Renaissance, Ramada International, and New World) and doubles Marriott's overseas presence.

Marriott International announces plans to merge its food service and facilities management business with Sodexho Alliance's North American operations, and to spin off to shareholders a new company comprised of its lodging, senior living, and distribution services businesses.

1998

As part of its long-term growth strategy, Marriott International spins off a new public company comprised of its lodging, senior living, and distribution services businesses. This enterprise adopts the MI name, Bill Marriott serves as chairman and CEO, and Bill Shaw is president and chief operating officer. Immediately following the spin-off, Marriott's food service and facilities management business (Marriott Management Services) merges with the North American operations of Sodexho Alliance. The merged company is renamed Sodexho Marriott Services, Inc. The "new" Marriott International continues the quest to become the preeminent hospitality company of the twenty-first century. Lodging properties grow to 1,500 with the opening of the Renaissance Parc 55 Hotel in San Francisco.

INDEX